Endorsements

Inspiring, insightful, and deeply practical, this book is an essential guide for women embarking on retirement. Drawing on extensive research and the stories of women who have redefined life after work, it offers a thoughtful exploration of the personal transitions that come with leaving the workplace. Each chapter provides personal stories, reflective exercises, and coaching-style questions designed to help readers uncover what truly matters to them, and create a personalized retirement map. Full of actionable strategies, this book will empower you to shape a rich, meaningful, and joyful future. An accompanying online workbook makes it a versatile tool for anyone navigating this pivotal life stage.

Gillian Jones-Williams
Founder of Emerge Development Consultancy and the RISE Empowering Women's Development Programme. Businesswoman of the Decade with the Best Businesswomen Awards

What Next? The savvy woman's guide to redefining retirement is an invaluable route map for women planning their post-work lives. Refreshingly, Jane Moffett's book does not try to offer advice on pensions, hobbies, and joining clubs but instead helps the reader navigate the next phase of life with ambition, self-awareness, confidence, and optimism. With the individual at its heart, this is not a 'one size fits all' approach to retirement but a flexible tool packed with hugely practical and reflective exercises which meet you where you are. Helpfully it explores relevant societal context, history, and theory which gives the practical content a really sound and relatable foundation. Written with empathy and insight it addresses fundamental issues that matter most.

Claire Williams
Ex-Managing Director of Inclusive Employers and attendee of the *Empowered Women: From Retired to Redefined* course

What Next? The savvy woman's guide to redefining retirement is a hopeful, optimistic read which speaks of the period post-retirement as an exciting stage of opportunity. Extremely readable, the book provides a comprehensive exploration of all of the relevant considerations for women as they approach retirement. The exercises after each chapter are a valuable resource for women to apply the learning from the book to their own lives. Well worth a read for anyone heading into this stage of life.

Professor Rebecca J. Jones PhD CPsychol
Professor in Coaching and Behaviour Change,
Director of the Henley Centre for Coaching,
Henley Business School

As a woman contemplating 'what next?' myself after a long career as a radio producer at the BBC, I felt both excited and inspired by Jane's book. *What Next?* underlines what a gift women of our baby-boomer generation have been given in being able to potentially enjoy up to another 30 years of productive life post-retirement. It highlights how important it is to reflect on how to make the most of this precious 'extra' time both in terms of self-fulfilment and in giving back to the community at large. It made me stop and think, and often shift my perspective as I was reading it. You might not realize that you need to read this book, but you will be very glad that you did!

Karen Holden
Freelance Radio Producer, 60 years old

In an ageing world, this is such an important book. Whilst statistics abound regarding the 100-year life, there is very little literature to help you actually plan for it! But there is this book, which offers women leaving work a guided coaching plan for designing their unique map of the future. Taking the reader through the psychological transition of 'retirement', it will help you plan your journey, craft your new identity, and give you hope for this exciting next stage of our lives.

Lucy Ryan
Managing Director, Mindspring. Author of *Revolting Women: why midlife women walk out and what to do about it*

What next indeed! With our 'squiggly' careers and our 100-year lives we are rethinking, reinventing, and redefining what retirement can look like. In this brilliantly accessible book Jane has created a practical tool to map out that process. First defining where we start, then figuring out our timetable, creating our own guidebook, deciding upon our travelling companions, selecting our travelling gear, and finally calibrating our compass! What a wonderful and much needed reframe – far from being a sad slide into obsolescence, our later years can be whatever we design them to be – challenging, fulfilling, thoughtful, thrilling, educational, or whatever combination we can dream up.

Emma Thomas
Executive Coach, host of Middling Along podcast series, founder of Managing the Menopause

In her thought-provoking book, *What Next?*, Jane Moffett offers women a fresh perspective on the post-retirement stage of life. She starts with an excellent description of the wider societal issues and asks important questions such as 'why is society not recognizing the power of women post-menopause?' and 'why is there no new vocabulary to describe this new life stage?' Through inspiring interviews and empowering coaching questions, Moffett also invites the reader to delve into personal questions about identity, purpose, and relationships. I highly recommend this book for anyone who is seeking to embrace the power and potential of the new life stage of 'redefinition'.

Berit Lewis
Author of *Ageing Upwards, a Mindfulness-Based Framework for the Longevity Revolution*

Many women such as myself have benefitted from rich and interesting careers. Our careers have nevertheless been hard-won and the prospect of letting go of this can be discomforting.

Before reading this book, I had found myself feeling 'untethered' and struggling to work out what I really wanted for this next phase. Right from the start, the book provided me with a reassuring sense of being understood and a sense of relief that the concerns that were swirling around in my head could be structured and made more coherent.

Moffett's research enables the reader to structure the issues she faces in a way that turns a sense of general unease into a clear set of areas for focus. For each area there are simple exercises, and for me these have provided a useful framework for reflection and have made navigating this transition a little less daunting.

Throughout the book, the tone is supportive and encouraging as Moffett helps the reader reframe and rethink this next stage of what she calls the 'breathing space years'. Whilst the book is well researched, it wears its theoretical underpinning lightly, and there are a myriad of useful references and resources for further reading and reflection.

Whether you follow the exercises step by step, or simply dip into them as the appetite takes, I would heartily recommend this book to any woman approaching the next phase of their life pondering the question 'what next?'

Sarah Jones
Former consultancy director, and coach, attendee of the *Empowered Women: From Retired to Redefined* course

I highly recommend this 'savvy' book, it provides an insightful and thorough context for the new landscape that the current generation of women approaching and entering retirement face. This background was really eye opening and emphasizes how very different the landscape is today for these women, the pioneers creating a new template for retirement.

The exercises and resources provided then allow the reader to work out what all of this means for them and what to do about it. The case studies drawn from the author's research bring it all to life and make it very accessible. I found the book a compelling read backed up by clear expertise in the subject and a very constructive approach. I actually think it's a must read for all generations as it opens up so many options for working life.

Rachel Goodwin
Leadership Coach, host of Wordwise Coaching Podcast

The savvy woman's guide to
redefining retirement

WHAT NEXT?

JANE MOFFETT

First published in Great Britain by Practical Inspiration Publishing, 2025

© Jane Moffett, 2025

The moral rights of the author have been asserted.

ISBN 978-1-78860-790-2   (paperback)
      978-1-78860-789-6   (hardback)
      978-1-78860-791-9   (epub)

All rights reserved. This book, or any portion thereof, may not be reproduced without the express written permission of the publisher.

Every effort has been made to trace copyright holders and to obtain their permission for the use of copyright material. The publisher apologizes for any errors or omissions and would be grateful if notified of any corrections that should be incorporated in future reprints or editions of this book.

EU GPSR representative: LOGOS EUROPE, 9 rue Nicolas Poussin, LA ROCHELLE 17000, France Contact@logoseurope.eu

Want to bulk-buy copies of this book for your team and colleagues? We can customize the content and co-brand *What Next?* to suit your business's needs.

Please email info@practicalinspiration.com for more details.

Contents

Foreword xi

Introduction 1

SECTION 1: THE LANDSCAPE 13

Chapter 1: Big life changes 15

Chapter 2: What's so special about now? 23

Chapter 3: The shape of women's careers 33

Chapter 4: Midlife collision 43

SECTION 2: JOURNEY PREPARATION 51

Chapter 5: Your starting point (leaving work) 53

Chapter 6: Your timetable (change in time and structure) 65

Chapter 7: Your guidebook (learning, growth and connection) 81

Chapter 8: Your travelling companions (relationships) 91

Chapter 9: Your travelling gear (identity, image and status) 105

Chapter 10: Your compass (meaning and purpose) 119

SECTION 3: YOUR MAP – THE SIX-PART DESIGN FOR YOUR FUTURE 131

Sara's map (fictional woman) 134

Your map 140

Acknowledgements 147

About the author 149

Resources 151

Notes 155

Index 167

Foreword

As a child of the 1960s and the daughter of immigrants I was taught that independence and freedom came from hard work. That focus allowed me to progress through my field at a pace so that by my 30s I was chosen as one of the 28 individuals working in the cultural sector to be a member of the first cohort of Clore Leadership Fellows. That cohort has achieved considerable career success, winning posts such as Director of Tate, Chief Executive of English Heritage, Director of the Van Gogh Museum, Chief Executive of the Scottish Chamber Orchestra, Artistic Director of the RSC. In my case, Director of Compton Verney Art Gallery, followed by Artistic Director at the Royal Academy of Arts, London. Those same Clore Fellows, now in their 50s and 60s, still talk about what they would like to be when they grow up. Finding purpose, feeling useful and fulfilled while remaining relevant and valid, is central to so many of our needs. It is even more complex when your identity has been wrapped up in what you do, as it is for so many of us. *What Next?* is an invaluable ally when trying to work through this conundrum.

As Moffett points out, having agency and control over our own destinies is important, however that can come with a fear of making the wrong decision. When in addition we feel that time isn't on our side, we become even more fearful of taking the wrong turn. When confronting this, I remember two things. One that a former Director of the South Bank Centre, London, told me when I was trying to convince him that he was making a mistake with a major structural change. 'Soriano,' he said, 'you may be right, but I'm going to try it and if it doesn't work... I'll change it.' The revelation that it did not need to be perfect, that things can be changed was earth-shattering. The second came from Moffett herself over a chat about my own future. Jane helped me to realize that I was thinking in terms of endings, rather than new beginnings.

Thinking back to my own beginnings, I remember the importance of supportive colleagues. It was no surprise, therefore, to read in these pages that a 2022 survey suggested that 43% of women believed that having a female role model in the workplace helped them to be more successful. I have worked hard to be that for others and have had the ultimate role model in nonagenarian Joan Bakewell, with whom I have worked these last 10 years on *Portrait Artist*, and *Landscape Artist of the Year*.

In 2014, at the age of 50, I stepped away from the Royal Academy and left behind a career of over 30 years with major institutions to set up my own business. I had always wanted to test my entrepreneurial abilities and soon realized that I wasn't alone. Many of my colleagues from museums and galleries were stepping away from their senior leadership roles but most were continuing to work independently. Myself, and many of those women, were initially part of the peer support group Women Leaders in Museums Network. As we stepped away from our positions, we formed a sub-group, SHIFT. The way in which they embraced the transition and new ways of working fascinated me to the point where I undertook a research project in 2023 examining their *Secrets of Success* (https://static1.squarespace.com/static/5d69261e9ec344000103f74e/t/64086cad7283c22c50982e41/1678273727983/Secrets+of+Success+Report+March+2023.pdf). How interesting, therefore, to learn from Moffett that the fastest growing group of entrepreneurs is women in their 50s.

There is much more to learn from Moffett's examination of this interesting time in our lives and the rich potential that it holds. It is an unsettling time for many of us. Too many unknowns, too many possibilities, but with Moffett's guidance we can start to make a plan.

Kathleen Soriano, Cultural Sector Consultant, Curator and Broadcaster

Introduction

When I think of someone retiring, it's a man.

WE'RE AT A time in history when a large cohort of women are at the life stage of reaching the end of their career, and of potentially leaving the workforce. Traditionally, the word for this stage in life is 'retirement', but is this word (with all its connotations) still fit for purpose? Taken from the French word '*retirer*' meaning 'to withdraw to a place of safety or seclusion', how pertinent is its use today?[1] How much do people leaving the workforce consider that they are 'withdrawing', and, if they do, what are they withdrawing from? They are leaving their workplace, so that can be seen as something that they are withdrawing from, but are they withdrawing from other aspects of their lives? Similarly, how many interpretations might there be to the words 'safety' and 'seclusion'? Safety could mean being in a place that feels safe to you, and could also mean spending lots of time with people you love, or who give you energy, or who make you feel like you belong (your own community of people), or it could mean drawing on your skills and experience from a life working, and using these in a different way and in a different environment. Seclusion could mean keeping yourself apart, or choosing time to spend on your own in order to recharge, to think, to decide on next steps.

Definitions of words aside, the way our society uses the word 'retirement' and the associations we make with it, often don't match the expectations and feelings of most people at this life stage. If this is so, then what should we be calling these years – the ones between someone being ready to leave work and live their lives in a different way, but not ready to feel 'washed up', redundant and sedentary? For the purposes of this book, I will be calling this life stage 'a time of redefinition', or 'leaving work', while also appreciating that many people will be going on to new work – be it paid or voluntary.

I see this time as one of opening out, embracing new things, reconnecting with things from the past, embarking on new adventures, accepting being older. It feels like it's about looking forward and looking back, while being very much in the present.

Because of changes in the law and in the way western societies perceive the role of women, many women will be approaching this period of redefinition in a different way, and with different expectations, to previous generations of women. This is a unique time, when women don't necessarily feel that they fit with society's image of someone who has retired. In an ideal situation they have economic independence, and feel young (in mind and spirit, even if not as much in body), and are ready for something else – something new.

If this description fits you, it could be that you've tried to find out a bit more about life after stopping work. Nearly every book that I found about this topic was written by a man (or a man and woman duo), and most case studies were based on the experiences of men. In contrast, this book is by a woman, for women, and I have set this important life stage within the context of being a woman in today's society, with many of the expectations that that might bring.

Who is this book for?

I have written this book primarily for any woman for whom work has been an important part of their life, and who is on the brink of stopping work – or has already stopped. It could be that you've stopped because you have decided that this is the right time for you to do so. It could be that you want a change in direction for this stage of your life –leaving paid employment in order to focus on a new project, for example. It could be that you have been a victim of gendered ageism (when midlife women are tacitly penalized for being female and older) and have been pushed out of the workplace and are unable to (or don't want to) find another job. It could be that a whole host of challenges (personal and professional) have come together at the same point, so that leaving work is the healthiest, best and only choice.

Whoever you are, I hope that you will find this book informative, helpful and inspiring.

Why me, why this book, and why now?

For the majority of my working life, I have focused on and researched different life stages that women commonly go through, and, more importantly, spent a lot of time listening to women's experiences, and finding ways of bringing women together so that they realize that what they're going through is not unique to them. Discovering that others might be going through the same experiences, or encountering similar challenges is incredibly affirming, and can help people to feel less isolated and more supported.

This book is one of the ways of bringing women together. The idea for it was sparked by a conversation with two good friends during a birthday lunch when the topic turned, as it typically does, to future plans. One of my friends raised her concern over what she was going to spend time doing once she no longer worked. She was the one who always had her career mapped out. As someone who changed job regularly, as is the trend in her industry, we had heard her say things like, 'I've got one more big job in me, and then I'll stop'. Now at the age of 59, she was looking ahead to the time after she worked. As someone with a highly successful, highly stressful and time-consuming career, she couldn't imagine filling lots of empty time, and she didn't have any hobbies that she could develop into something more meaningful.

Over the next few months, I kept going back to our conversation and could really see how she might feel that she was on the edge of a precipice when she decided to stop working. I kept having this image of her standing on the edge with nothing but a big drop ahead of her, and I couldn't see where she was going to get her zest for her future life from.

This inspired me to find out more about the experiences of women of my era – women who had found work to be important to them, who had maybe gone to university in the late 1970s and 1980s, who might have had successful professional careers, and who were considering stopping work. It feels like now is absolutely the right time to be writing a book about this, not just because I'm in this cohort, but because for the first time in the UK we are on the brink of having a large number of women who will be stopping work. In previous generations, working women tended to stop their careers when they had their family (although, of course, there were exceptions to this); this is not the case with my generation.

When I turned to the literature to read what the common themes, challenges and questions are for women in this situation, I realized that nearly all of the available books have been written by men, or have the model of men retiring in mind. There was nothing that I could find at that point that was specifically written for this group of women – my group of women. Discovering this propelled me to get going with my research and to interview women who had either already stopped working, or who were planning to stop working. Once I started talking about this to other women, it became obvious to me that writing a book about this could be beneficial to women going through this transition, so that their feelings and experiences felt validated, they felt less isolated in these feelings and experiences, and so that they got ideas and inspiration from other women going through the same thing.

This book is a product of all that I have learnt – through reading, researching and listening. I have used the stories of the women I have spoken to, and, at times, have used their actual words. All of these have been anonymized and used with their permission. Unless otherwise attributed, the quotes at the beginning of each chapter are taken from the interviews and conversations that I have had with the various women who have contributed to what I have learnt. I hope the book will be a useful tool for you, and one that you will share with other women at this stage of life.

New beginnings

In their book *The 100-Year Life*, Lynda Gratton and Andrew Scott address the fact that life expectancy is continually rising, and question the accepted concept of the three-stage life of education, work and retirement.[2] If there is a high possibility of living up to a further 30 years from the time of stopping work, how will people thrive (and I'm not talking just about finances here)? They believe that the interlinking of 'age' and 'stage' will become something of the past, that the focus will need to move from being 'older for longer' to being 'younger for longer', and that we will all need to continue to be active in order to get the most life satisfaction and to slow down cognitive decline. It will be a multi-stage life.

Part of their proposal for the way of living younger for longer – which they term as 'juvenescence' – and managing the years after leaving full-time work, is to invest throughout life in what they call 'intangible assets'. They categorize these under three headings: productive assets (associated with skills, knowledge, mental agility, empathy, creativity and innovation), vitality assets (to do with mental and physical health and what is needed to achieve this), and transformational assets (with the emphasis on self-knowledge and having a diverse network). Elements of these intangible assets are present in all the Blue Zones – the places in the world where there are the highest number of centenarians.[3] This is a whole new way of thinking about age, and completely counter to the image of a retiree who spends the majority of their day being sedentary and of thinking of this time as their 'twilight years'.

I'm now firmly of the belief that women of my generation have been gifted these extra years – a time of redefinition between stopping work and feeling like really slowing down – and that this can be an exciting (and daunting) prospect. As we are living in a time when life expectancy is increasing, and there is an emphasis on wellbeing (both physical and emotional), it could be that taking some time to really think about what is best for you right now could be beneficial. By reading this book and working through the exercises, or by joining one of my 'Empowered Women: From Retired to Redefined' courses, you will be investing in yourself, and gifting yourself this time. It could be that you're excited about this stage, and are relishing every moment of your time, or it could be that you're feeling apprehensive about the change that this time will bring, or are struggling with your new reality.

This time that you've been given provides the chance to do things you've not done before, to follow your passions, to redefine yourself. It gives you the opportunity to choose how you spend your time, what you put your energy into, what you add value to, and how. To leap into the unknown, to redefine this time of your life when you have vitality, determination and a new perspective on your life. As Herminia Ibarra describes in a podcast interview, this is a time of many potential pathways and 'the destination is often unclear'.[4]

Think of giving yourself breathing space – both in the short term to get you to a place where you can design the next years of your life to suit you, and in the long term where you can get the most from these years that have been gifted to you in the way that they weren't gifted to women of previous generations. By following the ideas, questions and exercises in this book, you will learn what you need in order to ensure that you make the most of these 'breathing space' years – they will help you to design these years to fit the shape of your life, your dreams, your aspirations and your potential.

What's covered, and why

Section 1 sets the scene. It starts with a brief look at the impact of big psychological changes (and stopping work is one of them), followed by a chapter highlighting some of the changes that came about in the 1970s which have affected young women who have been born since the late 1950s. I wasn't aware while I was growing up of how different this era was to previous ones, and how I would have completely different opportunities and expectations from those of my mother and her generation. I also didn't realize how this would affect the environment of the workplace.

Women's career development theory (the various factors that women take into account when making career decisions), the impact of having a family, the role of being a carer, and the collision of various events in midlife are explored in Chapters 3 and 4, as these frame the situation for women who are approaching stopping work.

Section 2 is focused on the themes that arose from the interviews and conversations that I have had with numerous women who have either left the workplace, or who are thinking about doing so in the next couple of years. When I spoke to these women, certain common topics emerged – things that they had found challenging or exciting, or things that they were anticipating would be tricky for them. These themes form Chapters 5 to 10:

- Chapter 5: Your starting point (leaving work)
- Chapter 6: Your timetable (change in time and structure)
- Chapter 7: Your guidebook (learning, growth and connection)
- Chapter 8: Your travelling companions (relationships)

- Chapter 9: Your travelling gear (identity, image and status)
- Chapter 10: Your compass (meaning and purpose)

In each chapter I have provided some information and insight as to why this feature of stopping work might be significant to some people, bringing in the experience of women I've spoken to. There are stories of what women have done, how they have approached things, and what discoveries they have made about themselves, which will provide inspiration and hope. Each chapter ends with coaching-style exercises and questions for you to work through, so that you can have a clearer picture of what you might need, and how you might approach things. The final section is your own map for the future, that you will have designed during the course of reading the book.

How to use this book

It's up to you how you use this book. You can read it from cover to cover starting with Section 1. Or, if that theoretical section of the book isn't for you, you can dive straight into Section 2. Each of the chapters in Section 2 ends with questions and exercises to help you to find out more about yourself. This is an opportunity to take time, to really think about yourself and what is important to you – what makes you tick, what you need to discard, what brings you joy. In Section 3 you will draw together all your work, adding in your answers to the key exercises (marked by stars) that are at the end of each of the chapters in

Section 2. You will then have your design for your own individualized map for your future.

There is also an online workbook incorporating the questions and exercises and a template of the design, which can be found at https://kangaroocoaching.net/from-retired-to-redefined. While this book is focused on women who are at the stage of leaving work, the questions and exercises would be useful for anyone of any gender.

Section 1: The landscape

SECTION 1 HELPS to set the historical, psychological and sociological scene of the stage of stopping work in the life of women. By finding out about the psychological impact of transitions you might increase your understanding of what is going on for you right now, and what you can draw on to help you. By having a greater comprehension of the historical and sociological forces that shaped this unique time of growing up and working that have led to where you are now, hopefully you will be able to put your own experiences into context and have a deeper appreciation of how your experiences might have been affected by these forces. By hearing more about the different life events that might come together for women in their midlife years, there might be things that resonate for you, helping you to feel a sense of commonality, and that you are 'heard'.

1: Big life changes

It took me a long time to come to the decision to stop. It was the most difficult bit.

You might be thinking, 'What's so special about this time of my life – everyone retires at some point?', or, like my friend, you could be thinking, 'I've worked since I was 15, how will my life be without any work?'. Or you could be somewhere in the middle. Whatever you're thinking, it's worth acknowledging that stopping work is a major psychological transition, and, as with all psychological transitions, you will be moving from a stable, known psychological state to an unknown state. You will be going from a position of knowing the rules, of being part of something concrete, of knowing the parameters, and having your own vision and concept of what this means to you, to a position where there are a lot of unknowns. This new territory is uncharted by you, won't have the same certainties, and you will have to discover your new vision. This could fill you with excitement as it can be viewed as a time of great opportunity. Or it could fill you with dread as it feels so unstable. It could be useful to think back to other significant psychological transitions, for example leaving school, leaving university, starting a job, changing your job, getting married, becoming a parent, bereavement or divorce. What did you feel then, what was tricky, and how did you navigate this stage? What did you learn about yourself that you can draw on now?

We know from the research that there is a link between decreased wellbeing and stopping work.[1] As with all changes there are gains, but there are also losses – in this case the loss of structure, of friends, of what you're known for at work, of your work title, to name a few. Some of these losses can seem on the surface to be about process and structure, and others can be deeper, to do with how you think of yourself as a person. This has shown itself in my 'Empowered Women: From Retired to Redefined' courses designed for women at the life stage of leaving work. There is an acknowledgement by the women that they are going through a transition, and that it will take time.

Because times of change can have such a psychological impact on people, various models have been devised to help explain what people might go through, and what could help.

The Change Curve

Developed by psychiatrist Elizabeth Kubler-Ross, the model of the Change Curve[2] can be useful to look at for any big life-changing situation. Here, the basic emotions of the original five stages of grief have been grouped into three transitional stages:

Stage 1: *Shock and denial.* After recovering from the shock of the change, people often go into denial – they might not want to face the change or may think that it won't affect them. These are very natural reactions, as our brains automatically view the thought of any new event that might destabilize the status quo as negative.

Stage 2: *Anger and depression.* This is a time when people try to find someone or something to blame, and can be accompanied by feelings of frustration or suspicion. This may then be followed by feeling low – feelings of apathy or isolation might be experienced.

Stage 3: *Acceptance and integration/commitment.* In this positive stage the inevitability of the change has been accepted. This is where new plans are made, accompanied by feelings of hope and a sense of new opportunities.

Having an awareness of the stages that people can go through when they encounter big changes can be useful in terms of explaining different reactions and feelings that might be experienced at different times. When thinking about leaving work, it could be that you're unable to think ahead to what life will be like – you're not ready to make plans (Stage 1). You then might have a period of feeling low, of not being able to summon up the energy to come up with ideas, or of feeling lonely (Stage 2). Finally, you will hopefully arrive at the point of feeling excited and full of energy and be able to think of the time ahead with optimism and a sense of purpose (Stage 3).

The Bridges' Transition Model

William Bridges, the eminent American organizational consultant, made the distinction between 'change' (something that happens 'to' people), and 'transition' (the internal process that a person goes through when they encounter change). The Bridges' Transition Model[3] is similar to the Change Curve, in that it focuses on the feelings that people might experience. Like the Change Curve, this model identifies three stages:

> **Stage 1**: *Ending, losing and letting go* – with the associated feelings of anger, denial, fear, sadness, uncertainty and loss.
>
> **Stage 2:** *The neutral zone* – this is where all the 'messy' work takes place, and which can feel uncomfortable and unsettling. It's the stage of psychological realignment that needs to happen between the end of one thing and the beginning of the next thing.
>
> **Stage 3:** *New beginnings* – once the necessary psychological realignment has taken place, people are ready to look ahead with positivity. They are open to opportunities, to new learning, to renewed hope.

With this model, there is a useful emphasis on the fact that any new stage also involves a sense of loss, and that, until this loss has been acknowledged and worked through (which can feel uncomfortable), what will be gained is not fully appreciated. For some of the women I've worked with, it became clear to them that loss was a natural part of the process of going through this life transition, but this hadn't been something that they had considered in advance.

The 4S Model

Devised by Nancy Schlossberg, professor of counselling who has written many books on coping with life transitions, the 4S Model[4] examines different factors that can be useful for people going through transitions. The 4S's are Situation, Self, Support and Strategies:

Situation – the trigger for change; is this within your control or not? With stopping work, this is all to do with who makes the decision, why they make it, and when it is made.

Self – having a sense of meaning and purpose, having a positive outlook, focusing on the self, being resilient.

Support – who you have around you who can offer support, on a personal and organizational level.

Strategies – creating plans. These could include choosing to act – or not to act, and using coping mechanisms such as reframing (looking at things in different ways, and using different language), focusing on self-care, modifying the situation (making changes that are within your control), devising ways to deal with the stress, and controlling meaning (being in charge of what the change means to you).

This model acknowledges that at times of transition people will be going through a lot of changes, and, by thinking about things from these four different perspectives, it can be possible to increase your self-efficacy – your belief that you have the ability to cope with this transition. There are strong links between these four components, and the key themes that have emerged from my research. For example, the manner of leaving work, and the reason for leaving (situation) can have a significant impact on how people cope at this time. The need for many people to find their purpose once they have left work (self) was seen to be key, as was the importance of relationships (support). Working out the importance of structure, deciding on what you need to function well in terms of learning and connection, and considering the changes in your identity and self-image (strategies) were also highlighted.

Let's take a look at the experience of Gillian, one of the women I interviewed, and apply some of these theories to her story.

Gillian decided to stop working because she was in her early 60s, so the timing seemed right. She'd seen colleagues who had continued working until quite a bit older and hadn't then been fit and healthy enough to enjoy the next stage in their lives. She definitely wanted to be in control of the decision and the timing; this fits with the 'Situation' aspect of the 4S Model. Because of the nature of Gillian's role, she needed to give 12 months' notice that she was leaving, and she recalled this as being a strange year when she subconsciously made adjustments, appointed her successor, and planned the next year knowing that she wasn't going to be there; she was in Stage 1 of the Bridges' Transition Model – the 'letting go' stage. Once she had left work, it 'hit her hard'. She missed the interactions with others and the rhythm of the days. As she said: 'It takes time to adjust. There are habits that have to be changed.'

At this point, she was in Stage 2 – the neutral zone. What helped at this point was giving it time, drawing on her own natural resilience and resourcefulness, support from her partner and friends, and choosing what she was going to invest her time in. As a consequence, three years after stopping work she described her situation as 'a lovely stage of my life'.

Looking at her experience through the lens of the 4S Model, we can see that she was strong in the criteria of self, support, and strategies, and that this really helped her move through this transition.

2: What's so special about now?

Throughout my career I fought for women to be seen.

BECAUSE THIS IS such a significant life stage, it could be useful to spend some time thinking about what brought you here to this particular point in your life, and what the backdrop is to this time for you. The next three chapters will help you to do this, and to realize that this is a unique time.

The contrast with previous generations

My mother was born in the 1930s when there was still a marriage bar in the UK. This meant that when women married they had to give up their jobs – this was the law. Although the marriage bar was lifted for teachers and by the BBC in 1944, and for the Home Civil Service in 1946, there were still jobs that you couldn't do if you were married. For example, you couldn't work at the Foreign Office (which didn't change its policy until 1973).[1] It wasn't until 1975, with the passing of the Sex Discrimination Act, that having a marriage bar was made illegal.

So, these women were growing up in a society that not only expected them to be housewives and mothers, but where they might not actually have been able to pursue the career that they wanted. Born in the early 1960s, I was part of the first generation of women who had greater freedom to choose a range of careers and jobs – like many other women of my generation, I had choice.

In the same way that there was much greater choice about jobs, there is now much greater choice about when to stop working. There have been several Pensions Acts since 1995 which have changed the age when UK citizens can claim their state pension (currently, this is at the age of 67), and, since 2011 the mandatory retirement age of 65 has been abolished. This means that anyone can continue to work for as long as they want – dependent, of course, on still having a job.[2]

With more choice come more decisions. While women of my mother's generation knew that they would receive the state pension when they turned 60, and that they would no longer be in a job, there are no longer these limitations – or assurances (depending on the way you look at it). In the past, apart from the self-employed, everybody retired at the same age (65 for men, 60 for women), and moved into the next stage of their lives – that of being a retiree (with everything society associated with that life stage). They had no choice about when to retire, but there was also a predictability about it – a 'cosiness'. Now, however, there is the choice (apart from in the case of redundancy, ill health or other circumstances), and it can be difficult to make the decision about when to retire – particularly when we may not feel we fit society's view of a retiree.

Of the people I have had conversations with, some have made the decision to leave their big, highly stressful jobs, only to go on to other high-profile and demanding work. Take Sadie, who, at the age of 51, moved from a top job in a very large institution, to run an associated charity. While she had left her initial career, she wasn't ready to stop working and still wanted to be employed doing something of meaning to her which used her skills, experience and contacts. Fast forward five years, and she has now come to the point where she is ready to leave this work and create a new life for herself. She considers herself to be at the stage of stopping work. Similarly, Paula left her corporate role when she was 54 and, rather than stop working entirely, she set up a business as a consultant, again using the skills, experience and networks from her corporate role. Seven years on she is ready to wind that up and do something different with her time which will give her greater freedom and won't tie her down.

On the other hand, Beatta decided to leave her work as a nurse, but, when it came to it, she realized that her job was so intrinsically linked to her sense of identity, that she changed her mind and continued working. A year on, she still isn't ready to make the leap to stop working and relinquishing her role and her title (see more about this in

Chapter 9 which focuses on the theme of identity, image and status).

In another example, Anna took a long time to fully come to the decision to stop work. She was so focused on not knowing what she would do with her time once she stopped working, that she couldn't move forward. Not having a plan and not knowing what her week would look like meant that she carried on working for longer than she might have. She did, however, find that it was liberating not needing to conform to a pattern of when she should stop work.

The impact of the Sex Discrimination Act

When the Sex Discrimination Act was passed in 1975, education was one area affected – it was now illegal for girls to be discriminated against by educational and training institutions.[3] This had a significant effect on the numbers of young women going to universities or polytechnics; in 1980, five years after this Act came into law, the proportion of females enrolling on undergraduate courses had risen from 35% to 40%.[4] There was, however, still a lot of sex discrimination within the secondary school system, including specific subjects for girls and boys (for example, home economics for girls, which was cooking, cleaning and sewing, and woodwork for boys), and different expectations – girls weren't expected to study sciences, for example (or certainly weren't expected to be good at them).

Going on to higher education opened more doors to a successful career. Although it was still a very small percentage of the population who accessed higher education, it was a lot less elite than it had been before. It meant that not just girls from the super-bright, highly privileged groups could access higher education, but girls from a greater demographic range could go – and at a time when there were no tuition fees, and maintenance grants were effectively means-tested, with a full grant covering all living expenses. The combination of these factors – the Sex Discrimination Act and access to free higher education – really helped to open up this path for more young women.

The impact of this was that those women leaving college expected to be able to get positions alongside their male counterparts. After all, they had studied alongside each other and had graduated with each other – so why not have the same opportunities of work – and be paid the same wage? However, sex discrimination in the workplace was (and still is) a reality, affecting recruitment, promotion and rate of pay. Despite the Equal Pay legislation of 1970, the issue of the gender pay gap continues in many professions and in many organizations – so much so that it has been mandatory since 2017 for large organizations in the UK to report data on their gender pay gap.[5] Since then, the gender pay gap has steadily decreased to 14.3% in 2023 – but this figure demonstrates that it still exists.[6]

So how did sex discrimination play out in the workplace, if it was no longer legal to discriminate in this way? This is a highly complex topic that includes some of the following: biases (conscious and unconscious), workplace culture, the predominance of male role models within many professions, the assumptions and realities of working if you're a mother, the glass ceiling, and traditionally male-only recreation activities and clubs (where deals, collaboration and job offers are made). To give an example, take the experience of women working in male-dominated environments, where the tacit expectation can be that you need to 'act like the boys' in order to fit in and succeed. One of my interviewees talked about becoming masculine in her approach, her language and her way of being. She said that throughout her career she had felt that she had had to be better than any of her male colleagues in order to succeed. Similarly, another woman said that three times as many men were up for promotion for senior jobs throughout her career, and that: 'We were still in a position where we had to throw more in than our male colleagues. We had the possibilities but had to work harder to achieve what we achieved. If you wanted to shine and get the promotion, you had to put more in.'

For both women, the lack of senior female role models made it much harder for them, and also perpetuated the image of a senior figure as male, so that the men they worked with didn't have their biases challenged. If all they were able to see at a senior level were men, then the assumption would be that women weren't capable of, or interested in, having senior roles. The few females that had managed to rise to senior roles were very much in a minority, which brought with it associated feelings of isolation and imposter syndrome – self-doubt. As recently as 2022, research has shown that 43% of women believe that having a female role model in their workplace would enable them to be more successful.[7] There's something very powerful about being able to see someone that looks like you – it helps you to believe that you too can achieve that.

Another impact of implicit sex discrimination is when the culture of the workplace is devised around the assumption that employees won't have any kind of childcare responsibilities. For example, if the employing organization has a long-hours culture with no flexibility, it's extremely difficult if you're a working parent with the main responsibility of organizing childcare – and this role predominantly falls to women. With the majority of nurseries in the UK closing at 6 pm, if an employee needs to get to nursery pick-up by this time, then they may well need to leave work earlier than many of their colleagues.

Someone I spoke to described how several successful and inspiring female bosses that she'd worked for were going to the supermarket in their lunch break to get nappies, and organizing the online shop – despite the fact that their husbands were at home.

The assumption that women are the ones who will work round their jobs in order to manage all things child-related was highlighted during the COVID-19 lockdowns, when it was found that with both parents working from home, and nurseries and schools shut except for the children of frontline workers, women were still doing more of the childcare and household management, and juggling their jobs around this.[8] So 'having it all' in reality usually translates into 'doing it all', with women doing a second shift of household and caring duties once they finish their day shift at work.[9]

What's the impact of all this when women come to stopping work?

There's the very practical impact of money to consider. Just as the gender pay gap is talked about a lot more, so now is the gender pension gap – and these two are related. How much a woman earns over the span of her working life can be significantly different from how much a man can earn because of the differential in salaries which still exists, and because taking time off work to have a family (including taking extended maternity leave, or a career break) impacts on career prospects. This then affects the amount that women are able to pay into their pensions. Also add to this the fact that it wasn't until 1990 that occupational pension schemes offered equal pension benefits to both women and men, that there are differences in the type of pension schemes that women and men participate in, and the way in which they are enrolled, and also that divorce settlements often don't take pension wealth into account.[10] The combination of these factors means that a 2024 gender pensions gap report found that, on average, women retire with pension savings of £69,000 whereas men retire with savings of £205,000.[11]

There's also the matter of what to do next. For women who have been trailblazers, who have worked hard throughout their career and have had a very clear purpose connected to work, stopping work, with the accompanying lack of pressure and stress, could be very appealing. Alternatively, the prospect of it could feel 'empty'. Having striven so hard to combine work with everything else outside work, will it be okay to relax and strive less now, or will there be the need to find something else that is purposeful? Maybe the need to achieve more is the reason behind the facts that, currently in the UK, the fastest growing group of entrepreneurs is women in their 50s;[12] there are increasing numbers of women in non-executive director (NED) roles;[13] many more women than men enrol in courses with the University of the Third Age (U3A).[14]

If you're someone who's thinking 'what next?' then this book is for you.

3: The shape of women's careers

(Work) is embedded in women's larger life contexts.[1]

What's so special about women?

WOMEN'S DEVELOPMENTAL PSYCHOLOGY recognizes the importance of relationships to women's growth and development.[2] This relationism, the fact that women's understanding of themselves happens within the context of their relation to others, extends to women's decisions when it comes to jobs and careers. They make relational decisions – decisions based within the contexts of the rest of their lives. Just as relationism is a common theme of many different career theorists, so is the fact that women's careers tend to have a different shape to men's. In contrast to the linear, steady and upward shape for the main part of many men's careers, women's careers have sometimes been called 'boundaryless', more fluid, determined by self-fulfilment and a greater emphasis on work/life balance.[3] Or like a 'kaleidoscope' in which women 'shift the problem of their careers by rotating different aspects of their lives to arrange their roles and relationships in new ways'.[4]

There is a view that women's careers consist of different phases – characterized by challenge, balance and authenticity – which often coincide with the early career, mid-career and late-career stages.[5] In the context of this book, the late-career stage is particularly interesting, sometimes described as a time of 'post-menopausal zest', a phrase coined by anthropologist Margaret Mead in *Life Magazine* in 1959. This is a time when women tend to have more energy, greater confidence, and a commitment to invest their time in something that they feel strongly about – are passionate about, even. It could also be that this time of 'authenticity' is delayed until after a woman stops working, as this might be when she has the time to dedicate herself to something that she feels excited about, or that she has always wanted to do.

Thinking about some of the women I have spoken to who had boundaryless or kaleidoscopic careers, there's Anna who had had a senior role as a director until she had a child. At this point she had a career break, and then became a part-time consultant working on a variety of projects. For the two years before she stopped work, she reduced her working hours to three days per week. There's also Sam who had been very successful during her 20s and early 30s, and was also a director at the time she had her first child. She then worked part-time for a while, and had another child; at this point her career was flatter in shape. When her youngest child was about three years old, she started working full-time again, and from that point onwards the shape of her career changed to more of an upward diagonal line again. Hannah, working in the legal profession, progressed quickly, becoming a partner in her 30s when she was pregnant with her second child. As her children grew older, she chose to work part-time as she felt she was missing out on too much. At this point, she had to resign from her post as a partner, so she left her organization and set up a business providing consultancy. All three of these women made decisions when they had children which impacted on their careers.

It's worth taking into consideration the different shapes of careers depending on whether or not you're a man or a woman, or whether or not you have had family or caring responsibilities that have influenced your career progression, as this might have an impact on how you feel during this time, how much it might affect you, and the reasons you might (or might not) have challenges.

Caring responsibilities

For many years there has been the nature-nurture debate: is who you are, what you like, how you behave, etc. determined by genetics, or the influencing factors of the environment you're born into and brought up in?[6] There is now a question mark over whether or not women do have more of a natural tendency toward caring and nurturing, or whether it is because of the way they have been expected to behave, have seen their older female relatives behave,

have seen most women around them behave. However, it is a fact that, in the UK, women still take on the vast majority of the caring that happens within our society.[7] Not just working in caring roles, for example nursing, social work and occupational therapy, but outside work – in the home and for relatives. This can take the form of caring for children, caring for elderly relatives and caring for partners who are ill, and all of these can impact on workplace work. The average age of working carers in the UK is 45–64 years, and a study by Carers UK found that a high majority of carers who were employed (79%) felt that their caring role negatively impacted on their performance at work, due to juggling these roles, and the impact of tiredness. They are also less likely to socialize with colleagues as they have less free time, so can feel isolated and lonely. When you think that one in six unpaid carers reduces their working hours or stops working altogether, and you put that together with the fact that the majority of unpaid carers are women, you can also see how there can be an impact on women's careers and the decisions that they make regarding work.[8]

The impact of having a family

I'd like to acknowledge here that not all women have children, and so this next section of the book might not be of interest to you. Please feel free to skip to Chapter 4 if you like.

For those women who do become mothers, this generally has an impact on their careers – even if this is only for a short amount of time (as seen in the cases of Anna,

Sam and Hannah). In the work I've done over the past 30 years I have noticed a change in the world of work, in people's expectations of work, society and colleagues, and of what is expected of them. However, there are still many fundamental things that have stayed the same. First, that women go through a deep psychological and identity shift when they become mothers; second that women still bear the brunt of domestic and childcare duties, and third that women are more likely than men to make adjustments to their work situations to accommodate the needs of their family.

In their book *The Birth of a Mother*, Daniel Stern and Nadia Bruschweiler-Stern identify three stages of the process of becoming a mother:[9]

1. still being at work while preparing for the birth of the baby;
2. when the baby is born and the period after when a woman is learning how to mother and isn't in paid work;
3. when the mother returns to the workplace – often as a changed person.

Psychologist Lynne Milward discusses how, in the period before maternity leave, the woman goes through some conflict with her identity – she is preparing for her new identity of being a mother while also working hard to maintain her valid employee identity.[10] When a mother returns from maternity leave, she has undergone a deep psychological shift – she is now a mother – and she needs to re-design her identity so that this new persona is merged with that of being an employee. One of the women

I interviewed for my master's dissertation (which was exploring the role of coaching at this time of returning to work), said that colleagues treated her as if she had just come back from a holiday or sabbatical, failing to realize or acknowledge the major life event that she had gone through, how her life had fundamentally changed. She described realigning her life and work priorities to adjust to her new norm and recognized the role that coaching had to play in providing her with the time and space to work through these shifts in her approach, outlook and behaviour so that she could successfully and positively reintegrate into the workplace.

Whatever the experience of women may be, all women who become mothers go through this deep and meaningful shift. At the time that I had my children, there was a division between those women that went back to work, and those that didn't (or couldn't). Either decision involved feelings of guilt or compromise: you felt you were either compromising your career, or compromising your mothering; you felt guilty that you weren't contributing to the family finances or fulfilling your potential and using the education and training that you had gained, or that you weren't doing either job (working and parenting) 'well enough'. Women that I've spoken to have talked about how, whatever you do, you question if you're doing the right thing, and constantly feel as if you have to justify your decision.

Caring for young children

In the last 50 years there has been a gradual change so that women are no longer expected to give up work in order to stay at home and look after children, although the speed at which this has happened is dependent on which country you look at. In the UK, Baroness Prosser's Review for the Women and Work Commission (2009), highlighted that women's potential in the workplace could be worth £23 billion and she set out recommendations that she believed would enable women to stay in the workplace.[11] Since then, there has been a push from the UK Government to encourage women back into the workplace after having children, as this has been deemed to be necessary for the country to run effectively, both from an economic and a societal aspect. This drive has been successful, with the majority of women returning to work, often on a part-time basis. However, as mentioned earlier, numerous studies have shown that in the UK, in a two-adult household comprised of a woman and a man where both adults work full-time, the hours spent caring and performing household responsibilities are much higher for women than for men.[12]

The impact of all of this on women and their work shows itself in many different ways. First, there could be the option of going back to work part-time to try to help with the struggle of combining the two roles of being a mother and being an employee. While this allows more time at home and can work well for lots of women, there are others who feel conflicted. I've heard lots of women say that they don't feel they're doing either job well and might choose to take a break from work to reduce this feeling of inner turmoil.

The lack of flexibility within some organizations can also make it impossible for women to continue with the jobs and roles they were previously doing. In 2019, I conducted a research project in the UK in which 421 women gave information about their experience of returning to work after a parental break.[13] Of those that hadn't returned to their previous job, 52% said it was because of a lack of flexibility (either of hours, or of place of work). As one woman wrote: 'There are flexible working and home working policies, however in practice, few managers are supportive.'

Some women find that it isn't possible to combine their work with having a family – either they work in a long-hours culture, or have a long commute, or their partner is away a lot with work, or their workplace doesn't accommodate working mothers. In some of my conversations I've heard women say that they decided to stop working because it was the best thing for the whole family unit. One woman described how she and her partner were pulled in too many different directions, and in order for the family to function well, she gave up work as this would be for the greater good of the 'team' ('team' meaning 'family' on this occasion). This decision to stop working wasn't necessarily an easy one for these women to make – they felt it was the right decision, but it was a big decision. Taking time out of the workplace often had an impact on how the women felt about themselves in terms of their self-identity, their confidence in themselves, their abilities (including that of having conversations) and their employability. Going from being in a role at work when they knew what was expected of them, were respected by others, and were part of an appraisal system, to a role looking after children where there is no 'outside' structure, no one telling them that they are doing okay, combined with a general sense of not knowing whether or not they are doing a 'good enough' job with their children, can include loneliness and feelings of loss – for example, of identity, self-esteem and confidence.

However, the time of not being at work, or working part-time, seems to have some benefits when it comes to stopping work. From my research for this book, I have discovered that many of these women have the confidence of knowing that they can carve out things for themselves outside work that have meaning for them and are enjoyable. Several of them also went through the transition from having a role that defined them in a way that had a certain amount of status attached to it, to having a role that was not of such a high status. Added to that, many went back to jobs that were less stressful, less demanding and less highly 'valued', so that there was 'less to lose' when they stopped this job. The lack of status from moving out of the workplace wasn't something that bothered them now, as they had already gone through this transition. For those women who didn't take time out of work to have children, however, the issue of a change in status and leaving a role that is generally highly valued could be more of a challenge when they stop working.

4: Midlife collision

Looking after my mum for 15 years stripped me of my free time.

'MIDLIFE COLLISION' IS a phrase created by researcher and author Lucy Ryan to describe the increase in the number of stressful things that can occur for women in midlife.[1] For women in their 50s there can be a perfect storm of events that all come together at around the same time, with the result that they can't see how they can continue working, and so leave their organization. It could be the effects of just a couple or several of the following: suffering debilitating menopause symptoms, raising teenagers, caring for parents, grieving for friends and/or family members, ageism, gendered ageism, or the impact of the COVID-19 pandemic on their thinking and what they realize they value about their life.

The recent increase in the dialogue about the menopause, with the accompanying discussion about what some women suffer, has highlighted the impact that this period of life can have on women in the workplace.[2] For many years the menopause was commonly referred to as 'the change', rather than the correct term being used – and, to me, this underlines the way in which it was rather casually disregarded. It is a time in a woman's life when significant hormonal changes are occurring, and although we had previously all heard of hot flushes, there wasn't much serious discussion about the other symptoms of the menopause – which can range from annoying to disabling – and how these can impact on work. As well as physical symptoms, a quick search on the common symptoms of menopause brings up anxiety, feelings of loss of self, loss of self-confidence, problems with memory, concentration and 'brain fog'. All of these can have a significant impact on how women feel – and behave – at work. Fortunately, the raising of awareness of the impact of the menopause on many women has led to greater discussion and debate, and to workplace training being offered, so that more people have a greater understanding of how their female colleagues could be affected.

However, there are still plenty of workplaces that do not offer this, and where women who are experiencing debilitating menopause symptoms feel like they have no other option than to leave work. They might not be ready to retire, and are certainly too young to draw their state pension, but, nevertheless, feel like they can't keep on going – can't maintain their current position at work. If they were supported during this time, their organization would benefit from the post-menopausal them – the wealth of their experience, often combined with energy, and a return of their self-confidence and sense of self.[3]

Another reason why women in their 50s might leave the workplace or reduce their working hours if they are self-employed, is if they are providing a lot of care for grandchildren, their parents or other relatives. An Age UK 2017 report highlighted that two fifths of grandparents who were 50 or older provided regular childcare help for their grandchildren, with 38% of this number providing care two or three times a week.[4]

With people living longer, it is not uncommon for parents to live until their late 80s or even into their 90s – and they typically can't manage completely on their own. For the person in the family who takes on a major part of the caring role (often a daughter), this can include from just a couple to many hours of care every week, and this can make it very difficult to continue working. A 2024 survey by the charity Carers UK highlighted that there are 5.7 million unpaid carers in the UK – this also includes caring for an ill or disabled partner, friend or relative, and, because the shift to providing care can be so gradual, many of this number don't view themselves as carers for quite a while.[5]

The feeling of wanting or needing to provide more care for their parents or partner, or wanting to reduce the stress involved in feeling torn between work and caring, was voiced by several of the women I interviewed. This often resulted in them leaving the workplace earlier than they might otherwise have done, but this decision didn't come without its concerns. At a time when they might have thought that they would be embarking on new ventures or adventures, and embracing the change in their lives that this period brings, some of them found that they had more things that they needed to take into consideration, and had less freedom. There was also a feeling that matters weren't necessarily under their control, and the fear that, because they no longer had work to fill their lives, they would be expected to invest a lot of their time in caring. Work had provided a logical boundary that then no longer existed, and there was uncertainty over how they might be able to create new boundaries to safeguard their time, while also providing care. For some of those women who needed to provide a lot of care for their partner, feelings of sadness, disappointment, fear and being trapped were voiced. Taking on a caring role might not necessarily have been part of their long-term plan, and there was a big sense of readjustment and uncertainty.

One of the themes that I hadn't expected when doing my research, was the impact of the COVID-19 pandemic on employees' decisions to leave the workplace. Often it wasn't actually during the pandemic that they left, but it was afterwards. The way they were treated, or the change in the workplace environment, was the tipping point for them. For example, one of the women I interviewed was a frontline worker (a Senior Practice Nurse). She continued in this job until 2021 but, due to changes in management, her autonomy was reduced greatly and communication became poor, making her feel she had little to say about important aspects of her role. She felt that the extra commitment to her job and her patients that she'd put in during the first part of the pandemic wasn't recognized or valued by the management, and so she chose to leave her job sooner than she had originally planned. For another, the change that the pandemic had created to the working environment, with everyone working from home meant that one of the big bonuses of work, that of social interaction – the being with colleagues – had been lost. She had already lost the thing that was most important to her, so the next step of deciding to stop working wasn't such a big one.

The impact of ageism

Ageism is when people are discriminated against in any way because of their age. This can take the form of not being considered employable over a certain age, or assumptions being made about someone's capability or about what they might want out of life, or whether or not they have much to offer to the workforce, all because of their age. While ageism is illegal in the UK, there is a huge gap between what organizations say that they do to support their older workers, compared to what actually happens (90% say they provide support, whereas only 5% actually do). In their 2023 study *Ageing Better? Life over 60 in the 21st Century*, the English Longitudinal Study of Ageing highlighted that 40% of the British population are over the age of 50, with this percentage predicted to rise.[7] If organizations aren't truly supporting their older workers, and drawing on their wealth of experience, then a shift in approach could be extremely beneficial and, indeed, necessary.

Learning and Development departments in organizations tend to focus their attention on training for employees in the earlier part of their careers, and recent research shows that older workers desire different outcomes from training.[8] While younger workers want to learn in order to help their progression, older people want learning for 'mastery' (to have a high level of skill in something), and to increase their self-esteem; in other words, there are different needs at different life stages. Being valued in the workplace is linked to having a higher learning goal orientation (that is, focus on developing competence by acquiring new skills, mastering new situations, etc.), and if people like what they do, and feel they can go somewhere within their organization, they'll still want to learn.[9] So, investing in designing learning programmes specifically for workers in the later stages of their careers could reap dividends – both for the organization and for the individuals. If, however, the reverse happens and organizations show disinterest in their older workers, or make them redundant, it can be very hard for them to get another job.

This was one of the things discovered by Eleanor Mills, former editorial director of the *Sunday Times*. Because of her experience when she was made redundant at the age of 49, she decided to set up an organization that would give hope to midlife women. In 2021 she founded Noon – a platform to support women from the age of 50 onwards – and its popularity is testament to how much this type of support is welcomed.[10] Noon provides inspiration, ideas, support and a jobs board in a bid to counter gendered ageism. Gendered ageism can manifest itself in many forms – for example, women being treated as if they won't understand things, not being listened to in healthcare settings and in the workplace. This is the topic of the book *Revolting Women: Why Midlife Women Are Walking Out, and what to do about it* by Lucy Ryan, in which she gives numerous examples of when experienced and competent women within organizations are 'invisible' to their male counterparts and overlooked for promotion.[11] Often, as a result of this, women may leave the workplace because they've simply had enough of being treated in this way – thus joining the ranks of women who have stopped work (not necessarily when they would have wanted to, though).

Internalized ageism is yet another factor that can affect those women leaving the workplace earlier than others.[12] This is when people might say 'I can't do that, I'm too old', or 'I won't be able to do that as I'll be too old'. We know that internalized ageism starts at an early age and is often determined by what a woman's mother or other key females in the family were like, and if they demonstrated internalized ageism. Internalized ageism can be countered by having a positive outlook on your own age, which is linked to a higher inclination to continue to work, or by having a female role model who works for longer. One of the women I spoke to talked about the strong role models of both her mother and her grandmother, and how this had shaped her attitude toward this stage in her life. At 93, her mother – who is an artist – still paints every day, and her grandmother was still writing plays into her old age. As far as this particular woman is concerned, retirement is 'not an option', and she firmly asserted: 'My age is irrelevant to who I am.' The vibrancy and vitality she exudes is incredible and inspiring – and is also contagious.

This is the end of the first section of the book, and hopefully sets the context for you and your experiences. It could be that none of this is news to you, or it could be that you have learnt something new. Hopefully you now have a greater understanding of the impact of wider societal issues on you and the stage of life you're at. The rest of the book is focused on the six elements that have been highlighted by other women:

- Leaving work (Chapter 5).
- Change in time and structure (Chapter 6).
- The importance of learning, growth and connection (Chapter 7).
- Re-assessing relationships (Chapter 8).
- Identity, image and status (Chapter 9).
- The quest for meaning and purpose (Chapter 10).

It's now time for you to start designing your own unique map for your future, and the next six chapters will take you through that, step by step.

Section 2: Journey preparation

SECTION 2 LOOKS at the six key themes that have emerged from my research. Things that have had an impact on lots of women, and may have been challenging. The themes are taken one at a time, and you will hear what the women I have spoken to have to say on each topic. There will also be examples of how people have navigated their way through the particular challenge that has emerged for them, so that you can see what others have done. The coaching questions and exercises at the end of each of these six chapters are designed to get you thinking about whether or not the challenges might be significant for you too, and to open your thinking so that you can decide what could be useful to you in the design for the next stage of your life. There is one starred exercise in each chapter that you're then asked to transfer to your final design – your map – which is at the end of the book.

5: Your starting point (leaving work)

I was battling with myself – do I stay, or do I go?

A LOGICAL PLACE to start is the time before actually stopping work. There are lots of decisions to be made when thinking about leaving: Why now? When will you leave? How will you leave? Who will you tell – and when? What do you need to put in place within your organization or workplace setting? If you're self-employed, what else do you need to consider? In talking to people, the phrase 'elegant exit' has emerged, and being able to manage this stage well is seen as important. If you're employed, remember this is only partly dependent on you because your organization will also play a large part.

What's in a decision?

According to the women I spoke to, one of the things that makes a big difference to people is whether or not they are in control of making the decision to stop work. Just like at other times of our working lives, if we're not able to be in control of big things that are happening to us, being able to have some smaller things under our control can make a real difference. For example, one of the women I spoke to told of how, due to a restructure, her job no longer existed and, instead, she was put on a project that wasn't very satisfying. This came at a time when she had given a lot of thought to whether or not to go from full-time work of five days a week, to four days; so, because she had no control over the actual job she had been assigned, she decided to take some control and reduce her hours to part-time. In this way, she was able to turn a situation round in her favour, to get back some agency over the situation, and to feel better about herself as a consequence. She explained: 'It's all about gaining the control. I've always been in control of my own destiny: What I do, how I respond to it, what I make of it is all up to me. It's my ultimate decision what I do.'

In a similar way, being in control over how and when you leave work is very empowering, and this resonates with the 'Situation' part of the Schlossberg 4S transition model, which is all to do with someone being able to predict or control how they navigate their way through a major life change.[1]

As mentioned in Chapter 1, stopping work can lead to a decrease in emotional health; this risk is increased if people stop working due to ill health or redundancy – they have lost their agency over the decision.[2] However, it's often not as simple as just deciding to stop working. Nearly everyone I spoke to about this said that they had spent a long time coming to the decision to stop, and that, when they finally did, it was due to a combination of reasons. Although age was a significant factor to their decision (and this was within a range of 55 to 66 years), it was not a 'given' as it would have been when there was a statutory retirement age. For these women it was because they felt they had reached a milestone (often turning 60), and it was more a sense of thinking about where they were in their lives, what they wanted to do next, and whether or not work was still important to them. As one of them said: 'I was done with it – the work. How long is life? I don't need to do this anymore.' For some of them, the significance of work had decreased, they had 'fallen out of love' with it.

In contrast to this, the importance of considering the years ahead was highlighted, and there was a definite link between age, health, and wanting to make the most of any opportunities that might come their way, or that they might create for themselves. There was the feeling of harnessing the energy and power that comes with being an older woman (but not an old woman) and being able to do things that hadn't been possible when working full-time, or even part-time. People had seen colleagues delay their time of stopping work, and paying the price of pushing themselves too hard, for too long, and then declining in health (or even dying) within a couple of years of retiring. As one interviewee said: 'I decided I didn't want to be one of those people who hangs on to the bitter end. That's not part of the plan.'

For some, this feeling was strengthened by the COVID-19 pandemic, as, for a whole variety of reasons (including being faced with a sense of their own mortality), many people re-assessed their lives – what they wanted and needed, where and how they wanted to live, for example. Questions such as, 'What am I doing? What do I want with my life?' surfaced for a lot of people. Through being furloughed some had had the chance to 'try out' life without work and found that it was actually alright.

As well as these internal factors, external factors also come into play when making the decision to stop working. Does your partner want to stop work, and want you to do the same thing so that you can do things together – or have they already stopped? Do your adult children need you to step into a childcare role? Do you need to provide care for a parent, relative or partner? As discussed earlier in the book, will your decision be a relational one? If so, how happy are you with that decision? When I was chatting about my research recently with a younger woman, she said that the timing of the arrival of grandchildren had really worked out for her mother, who had stopped working at the family business at the time when she became a grandmother, so she was able to help out with childcare. At the same time that she said that it was really lucky for her mum, she also questioned whether or not anyone had actually asked her if that's what she had really wanted to do!

There are also financial matters to take into consideration. While some of the women cited being in a healthy financial state (or benefitting from redundancy payments) as a factor to them stopping working, not everyone is in that enviable position. With the cost of living, and the increased life expectancy (with the prospect of living for many years after 'retiring') many people need to make the most of the time when they are still fit enough to work – albeit in a different role to one they have done before. Leaving a stressful, full-time job, or a job that is no longer possible because of its physical demands, but still needing some kind of income, means that a lot of older people are now working part-time once they officially retire. Well-paid part-time work, though, is hard to come by, and people aged over 65 are the second-largest group to be on a zero-hours contract.[3]

If you're self-employed, the decision to leave could take much longer to come to. You will likely have spent your self-employed years chasing business, making sure that you have enough money coming in, keeping an eye on your work pipeline, looking for opportunities, and saying 'yes' to things that might not be part of your normal remit because you don't want to let opportunities go. How do you then start saying 'no', and how far ahead of leaving do you need to decide to not take on any new business? It could be that this happens naturally – that you come to the end of a project, for example. I spoke to one woman who had been a consultant, who described her work as gradually tailing off. She said: 'Stopping just happened. It was lovely.' She didn't need to be proactive with her decision-making, unlike others who have to draw a line in the sand and say, 'This is the date that I will stop working and close my books, so I need to decide what date I stop taking on new work and what date I tell my existing clients that I will be stopping'. It can feel daunting, but taking a step-by-step approach can make it seem less overwhelming.

How will you leave?

Once you have made that mental shift and made the decision to leave, there are other things to take into consideration – both practical and emotional. First, there's the matter of timing. When is the best time for you to leave, and when is best for the organization? Thinking about what you have planned next, whether or not there is a time of year when you normally feel less positive, and what other people who are important to you are doing, are all worth weighing up. If you have a tendency to feel gloomier in winter, for example, then planning to leave in the spring might work better for you. Someone I spoke to greatly regretted leaving work in January, when it was harder to get enjoyment from gardening and from walking, which were two of the things she really took pleasure in.

Then there's the matter of how much notice you need to give – or will choose to give – which can be a tricky one. It's great to give yourself plenty of time to hand your work over, to ensure that you leave 'well', on your own terms, but this can be difficult to balance with how you think you may be perceived by your colleagues and your organization once they know that you're stopping work. If you think that you'll effectively be 'written off' as too old, not engaged or not committed, then this could be a reason to leave it until the minimum notice period; this was certainly one of the reasons for delaying stopping work cited by some of the women I spoke to. Once you even mention the idea of leaving work, how will others behave toward you, and what will they be thinking about you? It might have been difficult enough for you to come to the decision to leave – you don't need the judgemental opinion of others to make this time even harder! In fact, you might need the support of colleagues – or your boss – in order to clearly outline what your role encompasses, and what needs to be conveyed to your successor. For someone I spoke to, the situation of how to leave well in a way where she felt that her work and her competence were respected, was the most difficult part of the whole process of her stopping work. She felt completely overwhelmed by the idea of how to convey the detail of everything she did, but was reluctant to involve her boss. She felt bad that she was leaving, aware of the work that it would create for others, and didn't want to create even more work for them before she left. Once she realized that it was essential to involve others, and told them about how she was feeling and what she needed, everything became easier. They had been completely unaware that she felt like this – like she was drowning – demonstrating how useful it can be to have honest conversations early on in the process. Taking some time at this point to decide what you need to do when, and what support you might need, could make this a much easier process for you.

Having a phased ending, gradually tapering down what they did by moving from working full-time to working part-time, or by reducing their part-time hours further, was very helpful for some of the people I spoke to. Not only does this start the handover process a lot earlier, enabling your employer to realize what they need to do to manage well without you, but it also gives you the chance to get used to being at work for less of the time. There is then not such a stark contrast between working and not working.

When it comes to the point of actually leaving, it's important that there is the chance to do this well – it's the final part of your 'elegant exit'. The benefits associated with leaving in a way that is supported, where your value to your employer and your contribution are acknowledged and honoured, are long-lasting and impact how you begin the next phase of your life. One of my interviewees had her final day planned out, which included taking time to say goodbye to and thank her team. She arrived at work on her last day only to find that her work pass had been cancelled – she couldn't even enter the building, let alone say goodbye to the people and the place. The feelings of sadness, disappointment and regret that this created clouded how she felt about her employer of 40 years.

What can you learn from…

Natalie

Having worked in a senior position in a fast-paced industry full of young people, Natalie had planned to stop working at 55 – although she wasn't certain that she would have the confidence to actually go through with this plan, as she loved her work so much. A few months before her 55th birthday, her organization went through a restructure, she was made redundant and had to leave the building for the final time three hours later. Initially she was in shock, but once she had got over this reaction, she was able to see that being made redundant had actually been helpful, as the decision had been made for her, saying: 'I took an opportunity during restructuring to do what I want to do.'

Although she hadn't been in control of the decision to leave (both its timing and how it had happened) she was able to turn the situation into a positive one by taking control of how she reacted to it and what she did next, and recognizing what she had gained from the situation. She had plenty of friends and was involved in lots of activities that were important to her and, a few months later when I spoke to her, she was really enjoying 'not being accountable to anyone else'.

She had been able to put some structure into her week, and, while she wasn't sure how she would feel long-term about not having the difference between work and the breaks that holidays give you, she had a level of self-confidence that she would work something out for herself. The fact that she is generally a very positive person who is very aware of how she approaches life and what she needs in order to function well, was really working in her favour during this big shift in her life.

Joanne

Having a health scare and being absolutely exhausted were what finally helped Joanne to decide to leave her career of 25 years. She had worked hard to succeed, and to be an effective female role model, but knew that this was the time to stop. Her overriding sense was: 'If I don't get out now, I'll just be defined by this.'

This jarred with her drive to be more authentic – and to fulfil what she sensed was the reason that she had been 'put on the planet'. She was able to list all the roles that she had been 'good' at, and added: 'but (I) haven't yet found the authentic person that I am.'

This drive to find her authentic self was what gave her the courage to leave – 'to jump'. She had been the one who decided to leave and had been in control of how it happened, and although she went on to do another full-time high-profile role in a different organization, this break away from her previous career, and the way she (and everyone else) had defined herself for 25 years, was a big step in enabling her to decide, seven years later, that she was ready to leave the workforce. She was then also able to be in control of this decision too, giving a long notice period, and being able to hand over to her successor in a timely fashion.

> ## Step 1 of your journey
>
> I promised you in the introduction that, by the end of this book, you would have your own unique map of your future. This is now the time to start designing that map. Complete the following exercises in as much or as little detail as is right for you – remember this is for you, and might only be read by you. If you would find it easier to talk through your answers rather than writing or drawing them, you could choose a trusted person to work with, or even dictate your answers into a device (for example your phone).

Your reasons

Draw a spider diagram to capture your reasons for leaving work:

Take a piece of paper and draw a circle in the middle of it. In this circle write 'My decision to leave'. Draw lines out from this circle, writing a reason at the end of each one.

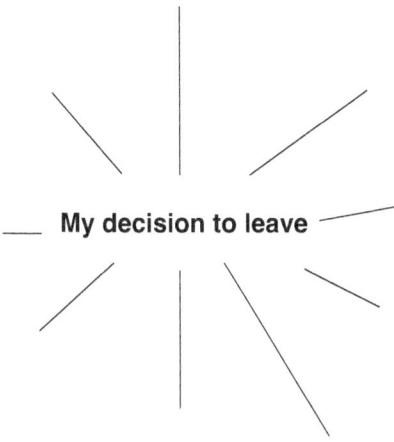

Take a note of:
1. how many different reasons there are, and why these matter;
2. which reasons are the most important to you.*

'Empty chair' exercise

Think about the person you are most dreading to tell that you are handing in your notice (if there's no-one you're worried about telling, then just skip this exercise). Set up two chairs opposite each other and, sitting in the first one and imagining the person in the other one, tell them that you are leaving. Now get up and move to the other chair, and imagine you are that other person and have just heard the words that you have said. How do you think you will feel as this other person, and how will you respond?

Your last day
Imagine your final day at work: What does it look like, who's there, what happens? What do you need to do to make sure that becomes reality?

*You will be adding this to your design at the end of the book.

6: Your timetable (change in time and structure)

When my life is more constant what will I do? I worry that I'll be lost.

So, you've left work, you've returned from the wonderful trip that you had been planning for the last year, and you're back home. Now what? In your mind's eye you have a long road stretching ahead punctuated by various events and projects, but where is the structure to this time, what are the kerbs or edges to this time, and why might you need them? Let's put this within the context of the fact that, on average, people are living longer. Currently, if you are 60, you have a 50% chance of living until 90 or older.[1]

It could be that you're facing 30 years after stopping work. If you think back 30 years, consider what you have done and what you have achieved since then! Fast forward another 30 years – while bearing in mind that you will slow down as you become older – and you can see that things have changed over the generations, and you might not be ready to sit in an armchair for the rest of your life (proverbially speaking). This is a time to work out in which ways you want to invest in your 'intangible assets' and make this time ahead matter.

I was recently at an event where someone asked me what coaching was, which gave me the opportunity to really think about what it is, and what people gain from it, and found myself thinking about it in terms of time. I often hear people say that coaching sessions have given them 'time and space' – things sadly lacking from daily life. Having coaching means that you create time for yourself in your diary, which you wouldn't do otherwise. In this time, you can 'hear yourself think' and have realizations. A coach can help you to clear the clutter that's in your head when you think about things, and the result can be to have clarity and, maybe, a plan. It's like having a tangled ball of yarn which, through the work you do in the coaching sessions, becomes untangled, straightened out and reformed into a neat, smooth ball. Putting aside the time when still working to have coaching in order to think about who you are, what you want, your values, what will be important in your life, and what will give you meaning and a sense of purpose, could reap its benefits once you're no longer in the workplace. Or, if it's not possible to have coaching, use this book instead. Because it's a guide that can be dipped into – or read all the way through – you can use any snippets of your available time to initiate important thinking and planning.

In this chapter I will be considering aspects of viewing and using time, and of the greater or lesser importance of structure in people's lives.

Time

For the majority of people of working age in the UK, there is a strange, unbalanced, attitude to time. During our working lives, because of the structure of the working week, it is hard to have a feeling of pace – of a measured sense of time that is calming. Instead, we tend to cram things in because of deadlines, having multiple tasks to complete, or so that we feel we're getting the most out of every day. Our leisure time can also be equally full, with plans for exercise, seeing friends, grocery shopping, trips to the cinema, theatre, exhibitions, concerts, etc.

As people are approaching the stage of their lives when they are no longer working full-time, their relationship with time becomes paradoxical. One of their concerns is how they will fill their time – it can feel like a never-ending expanse stretching ahead of them, which can be frightening. When faced with the prospect of arranging regular activities, however, they often don't want the commitment. After spending decades of not having the freedom to do what they want when they want, they don't now wish to be tied down. Although there could be the desire for structure, there needs to be flexibility. You hear tales of people who, in the anxiety that they will be bored and will be faced with a massive void when they stop work, throw themselves into lots of activities – trying out whatever comes their way – and thus over-committing their time, with the result that they find themselves too busy.

These concerns about the time ahead are set within the context of working, and not feeling that there is enough time to plan and think ahead. A common theme when talking to women who are still working is that, while they were concerned about what they would do with their time (to ensure that their lives had purpose and meaning), they couldn't find the time to do the thinking that would be useful for working out what will be important to them – the stage that needs to be worked through before any future planning can happen.

When I think about what I like to do when I have the time – spare time, relaxation time, down time – I can come up with a list which includes walking, kayaking, reading, gardening, singing, seeing friends, exploring new places and revisiting old favourites. This time is squeezed in or is planned for – timetabled into my diary to fit round work, or as a deliberate decision of what to do when I am on leave. However, when I think about all of every day being filled by these activities that I find pleasurable, I know that I will feel dissatisfied – a bit aimless, purposeless, discontented. That sounds incredibly privileged (and it is), but I know myself well enough to know that I need to feel that I am doing something 'concrete' that will be satisfying to me. This is why, for me – and, I think, for a lot of other people – having 'hobbies', or relying on these hobbies, won't be enough when I stop working. I will need to do more, which is something I explore further in Chapter 10.

However, if you know you're someone who is absolutely going to relish that time of not being rushed, of being able to pace yourself doing the things that you love – rather than packing these things in around the time available to you when you're working – then this may be a much smoother transition for you.

Whoever you are, and however you view this new phase of your life, you will almost definitely have had plenty of advice from friends and acquaintances – everyone has a view! As someone I interviewed said: 'Some people warned me against putting in too much, others said to try anything so that I could see what I liked.'

Another woman I spoke to said: 'When I stopped is when I would work it out.' She knew that she didn't have the headspace (or time) to try to work out what she would be spending her days doing once she was no longer at work, and she was happy with knowing that the period of time straight after stopping would be about experimentation, feeling and finding her way. Similarly, someone else said: 'It's difficult sometimes to envisage what it will be like.'

Another woman was told: 'Don't rush into anything else. When you're not yourself it's easy to pick the wrong thing.

Give yourself some space.' This was echoed by the advice: 'Don't do too much too quickly because you could find you're doing too much.'

You will know yourself what you need, so take all advice with a pinch of salt, and don't worry that you might not do what others have done.

One of the common concerns raised by the women I interviewed was that they didn't want to waste this precious time, this breathing space, this time between leaving work and feeling older and of retirement age. They wanted to make the most of still being able to do all the things they wanted to do. They didn't want to look back and have regrets about not making the most of this time. It could be that, when at work, you love to pack everything into the time you have – or you might like to pace yourself, ensuring that you're not feeling rushed, and devoting as much time to each thing as it needs (although you might find you 'do' fewer things than another person who packs it in). The feeling that I got from the women I interviewed was that they could actually give the time that was needed and that they wanted to give, to the things that mattered to them. For example, several women mentioned wanting to stop working so that they had more time to care for elderly parents. They no longer wanted to squash this in around work. Making this positive decision to 'give back' time to their parents in this way meant that they felt less stressed and that they had agency over the caring that they did. They were making the choice to spend this time, rather than it being forced upon them.

Structure

Recent conversations with one of my daughters who is a primary school teacher, have reminded me of the importance of structure for children. The fact that they know what they'll be doing at each point of the school day. Its predictability, and the security that that brings, means that they feel safe and 'contained'. There are lots of ways of creating containers in the psychological sense, but what they all have in common is that they provide a 'holding' space in which people are able to feel safe and secure.

For many people, this holding space is provided by working. There is a structure to their working day, week, year; they know what to expect, and when. There is also the benefit of having clear boundaries – when they're at work they're working, and when they're not at work they're in their leisure time (which might, or might not, be structured). For the majority of people in the UK, this all changed during the lockdowns of the COVID-19 pandemic, as they were no longer able to go into work unless they were a frontline worker. This meant that the physical boundary between the workplace and the home was no longer there, so it was much harder to maintain the boundary between working and leisure time. It was so easy just to check your emails in the evening and respond to them when they were in your mind, and much more difficult to be disciplined about not looking at any work-related things after work hours. For lots of women in particular, this blurring of the edges, and the lack of definite boundaries between work and leisure time, resulted in a decline in mental health.[2]

I wonder at what point losing the certainty of structure – which, for example, is provided at school or at work – is an advantage to some people? When I think of all the people I know, some of them thrive on spontaneity and not having structure to their day, and others (more people) thrive on having structure – knowing what they will be doing, and when, and what is expected of them. One of the things people who work full-time love about being on holiday is the freedom that that time offers – the lack of structure to their days. But what about when this is all the time, when there is no shape to your days or weeks or months? How much is having control over your days, or having the familiarity of having a shape to your days linked with your mental health? At what point does the luxury of not having to wake up to an alarm clock fade, and make the day seem a bit pointless? Research shows that there is a link between having regular patterns and physical and psychological health. For example, waking up at the same time every day is helpful for maintaining our circadian rhythm (our natural 24-hour cycle). Also, having a pattern to the day gives a sense of familiarity which can reduce stress and give a feeling of having more control over our lives.[3] This could be particularly key if the decision to stop working is out of your control; once the pattern of work is no longer there, it's possible to 'take control' of the new stretches of time by creating a structure to the day that is right for each individual.

Putting structure into your day or week, however, can be difficult to balance with the desire to be spontaneous and can sometimes create some internal friction. It could be useful to view structure as one of the things you might desire depending on what else might be on the horizon or on offer, rather than as being an absolute timetable to be adhered to at any cost. Another potential rub is when you have things that you want to put into your week which are just for you, and you also have caring duties. It can be hard to give yourself permission to take time off for yourself, with the feeling of 'how can I allow myself to do this when it means that I will be spending less time caring?'. Recognizing that your own needs are valid, and working out what these needs are, is an important area to address; if you don't look after your own needs, then there may come a time when you won't be able to look after the needs of others.

There's no right or wrong approach to this. I heard a wide range of views about structure in my conversations with women, including:

> It's very easy to get into lazy ways, just doing nothing – nothing concrete.

> Maybe I don't have enough structure now.

> I like getting up and thinking 'what can I do today?' I enjoy this, but I also wonder if this is okay.

> I push against structure. I'm very happy without structure.

It can be useful to spend some time working out what you need to have in your life in order to flourish, and not to flail. Which one of these people are you, and what does that mean to you in your time after work? If you're someone whose job is very structured according to the time of year (for example, teachers), then it could be important for you when you stop working to think about what you will be doing in September when the school year starts. One of the women I interviewed worked in education; she stopped working in July at the end of the school year, and, although she had a big trip planned, it wasn't until January that she went on the trip. That period of time between September and January was really tough for her. She hadn't had her time away to make the adjustment she needed to make to the rhythm of her life. She just felt like something was missing, as she couldn't help but think about what that autumn term had meant to her for the last 40 years, and how it had set the rhythm of the academic year.

What can you learn from…

Faye

When I asked Faye to sum up her life now that she has left work, she said: 'Good. Very good. Busy.'

It was great to hear that someone who had had such a full-on job as a Senior Practice Nurse was relishing her life now. Before stopping, her family had urged her to do less, worrying that the way she was living her life was bad for her health. Now that she had stopped working, she really appreciated the fact that she was no longer rushing around. However, she had created structure to her week, and her diary was planned – she made sure of that. Her week now includes visiting her elderly father, spending time with her children and grandchildren, going to the gym regularly, meeting up with friends and previous colleagues, and giving herself permission to 'just sit and read'. She relishes the extra time she has, and being able to just sit around for a few hours if that's what she chooses, and this is all done within a structure of her own creation.

Stacey

For Stacey, previously a retail consultant, her answer to my question about what the best thing was about stopping work was: 'Time is the biggest benefit. Time to think about what I want to do and do not want to do.' This, despite the fact that her biggest concern before she left was: 'How am I going to fill that time? What does my week look like? What am I actually going to do with myself?'

It completely suits her personality to be spontaneous and not have a routine. She loves the fact that no two days are the same. Like Faye, she's given herself permission to do things that she would never have done before – like spending time during the day reading a book – and to go with the flow and not have structure. The time she gained from not working has allowed her to spend time with her ageing mother, and to do the things she wanted to do for her. Previously, she had felt guilty all the time – having to make decisions between attending a meeting or talking to her mother. She also mentioned her consciousness of her own age and very clearly believed that you have to enjoy the time that you have got.

Step 2 of your journey

Complete the following exercises in as much or as little detail as is right for you – remember this is for you, and might only be read by you. It will, however, form part of your design for your future. If you would find it easier to talk through your answers rather than writing or drawing them, you could choose a trusted person to work with, or even dictate your answers into a device (for example your phone).

Your Wheel of Life

It can be useful at any time of life to take a step back and review what you spend your time on, compared to what you would like to spend your time on. If you are planning to stop work, this is your chance to have a really good think about how you want the balance of your life to look; if you've already stopped working, here's your opportunity to see if you've got it right for you at the moment.

Time

1. Look at this list and choose the eight things that are most important to you to spend your time doing (please feel free to add to this list so that it is accurate for you):

friends	family	health	holidays
fitness	caring	fun	relaxation
community	work	hobbies	volunteering
adventure	creativity	exploration	spirituality

2. Draw a big circle and then add four lines to it that cross in the centre to form eight spokes:

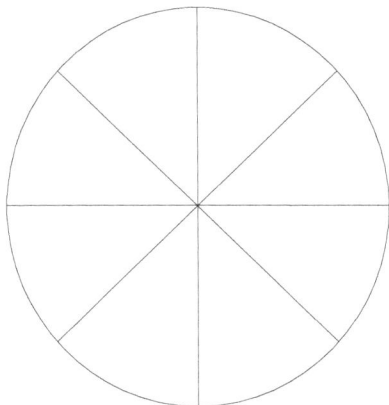

Label the end of each spoke with each of the eight categories you have decided on.

If the centre of the spoke is 'no time at all', and the edge of the spoke is 'masses of time', plot how much time you want to spend on each of your eight categories.

3. What do you need in every: day, week, month?

What does this tell you?

Structure
How important is structure to you in your life on a scale of 1 to 10?
(1= not at all important, 10 = very important)

How much do you enjoy going with the flow on a scale of 1 to 10?
(1 = hate that idea, 10 = love it)

Your plan

If you knew that you only had ten years left to live, what would you want to do/make sure that you did?

If you knew that you only had five years left to live, what would you want to do/make sure that you did?

If you knew that you only had one year left to live, what would you want to do/make sure that you did?

Reviewing the above, design your plan for the first week, month and year after stopping work (or next week, month and year if you've already stopped).*

Here's an example of this type of planning:

Week 1:
See friends at least three times.
Do some exercise at least twice.
Go for a walk every day.
Go out in the evening at least twice.
Spend time thinking about what I want to learn/continue learning.
Do some gardening at least twice.

Month 1:

Reconnect with at least two people from the past.

Go away for at least a couple of days.

See a new film or play.

Go to a concert.

Clear out the back bedroom.

Complete my first gardening project.

Research opportunities for me to use my skills and experience in some way.

Year 1:

Expand my network of friends/people I spend time with.

Be fitter.

See real progress in my learning.

Have two long trips away (of at least three weeks each).

Have a plan for my next year.

*You will be adding this to your map at the end of the book.

7: Your guidebook (learning, growth and connection)

> *Keeping up to date with what's new and happening. Not to be irrelevant, taking up space and resources, but to be a contributor of some sort.*

WHEN THINKING ABOUT learning and keeping skilled, increasing one's knowledge, having mental flexibility and agility, keeping healthy and having a well-functioning brain, and being open to new experiences and learning, are all part of the intangible assets identified by Gratton and Scott (see p. 7).[1] In fact, they reframe the phrase 'recreation time' to 'time to re-create', believing that at different stages of our lives we need to invest time (either at the weekend, during annual leave, or once we leave work) in re-creation – to re-create ourselves by learning new skills and updating existing ones. By always having an eye on the future in this way, we are then able to make the most of any opportunities that come our way. I have found it interesting in the many conversations that I have had with women, how many of them have stressed how important they think it is to be involved in new or continued learning. This isn't something that they feel duty-bound to do, it's more that they have a desire to keep engaged and vibrant.

Why bother – what's in it for you?

The facts of the matter

We know from the latest research into neuroscience that we can continually 'grow' our brains – we have the ability to learn new things and lay down new neural pathways. And the more we do of one thing, the stronger that neural pathway will become.[2] During our working lives we are often in a position to attend training courses, learn new skills, attend conferences, hear interesting speakers, etc. We do this – or are encouraged to do this – because it will help us to develop, be promoted and reach the next level, and research shows that the desire for progression is the main motivator for younger workers.[3] The same research shows that older workers are motivated to keep on learning to get higher levels of self-understanding, self-esteem and 'mastery'. No longer are they engaging in training in order to progress, but for much more personal reasons – for internal validation, the desire to get better at things for their own sakes. And the greater a person's self-awareness is, the greater the potential of achieving optimal self-development. Other research also shows that there is a link between retirement planning and being motivated to develop and master new skills (otherwise known as learning goal motivation).[4] From research on ageing we can also learn that another great advantage of keeping your brain alert – thinking about it as a muscle that needs to be exercised – is that it can help lower your risk of developing dementia and help to keep your brain younger.[5]

Just as you wanted (and needed) to continue learning when at work, it doesn't make sense to stop learning new things once you leave the workplace. This is a stage of life when you have more time, when you can (hopefully) choose what you learn about, indulging in learning for learning's sake, and about something you're really interested in – rather than doing training in something you've been recommended to do. Also, if you're no longer in a position where you're having to use your brain in the same way as you do at work, it's important to keep on challenging yourself in terms of your thinking, to ensure that you don't become too 'settled' in the way you think, or avoid thinking about things from different perspectives. One of the things that women doing my courses most appreciate is being in a group of other people that they don't know who are at the same life stage but coming at things from different perspectives. This range of viewpoints and outlooks means that questions are asked from a variety of different angles, and this increases creativity in thinking, opens up the mind and leads to new insights.

Learning and development in practice

There is a lot of investment in the learning and development of the younger members of the workforce, with much less opportunity for continued professional development being offered to older women – a fact pointed out by Lucy Ryan in her book *Revolting Women*.[6] When you think about the benefits of adding new learning on top of years of experience, it simply doesn't make sense for older women to be neglected in the workplace. Combined with all the conversations I've had with women who highlight the importance of continued learning to them on a personal level, this got me thinking about learning and development in the context of not being at work anymore.

In the conversations I've had with very creative people, they are convinced that we all have creativity or hidden skills within us, but that we might not have found the way to express this yet. They are firm believers that if you come across an opportunity to try out something new that appeals to you, then you should take it. By not attaching too much pressure and expectation to this, it's possible that a whole new passion could be unlocked. One of these women described always having her 'outlet of joy' – her creativity – and gradually spending more time on this so that once she stops her main job, she can focus even more on it.

Whether or not people feel that they are creative, the desire to continue with learning was one of the key themes that came out of my research. It was something that the women I interviewed didn't want to stop doing and were excited about continuing – but without the pressure of their jobs. For some, it was the feeling of excitement because of having the combination of time, good health and interest in things: 'I'd like to feel that there's something I haven't yet done that I have a go at – something new.'

For others, it was linked to their sense of purpose and still having relevance: 'I have to feel that I've still got a place in the world.' For another, the desire to continue to challenge her brain was just that – a continuation, as she identified that she is someone who has always been curious: 'Keeping my mind fed and challenged is important to me.'

She had come to the conclusion that she wanted to learn new things that are interesting – relatively complex, but not stressful – and that learning and thinking are an integral part of her life that she wanted to continue. Someone else firmly believed that it's good to experience a variety of things, as you might not find what you need until you're exposed to it. She also thinks that we all have hidden skills that we might not even know that we have. And someone else said: 'I'm more interested in learning new things.' For her, it is this exploration of new things that gives her excitement.

Keeping connected

I've also noticed that a common concern among the women I've spoken to is connected to where they will get their stimulation and inspiration from – the thing that gives them energy – once they're no longer at work.

A few women identified that it was being with younger members of staff; being involved in their conversations, finding out about what they think about things, the music they listen to, the language they use, how they spend their spare time. This meant that they felt 'current' or, at least, aware of what is live for young people – which, in turn, helps them to feel younger and connected with contemporary culture. For another woman, it was having stimulating intellectual conversation with peers in her field, thinking about new developments in other areas and how she could use this in relation to her industry. She found that this new learning challenged her thinking and led her to consider what she needs to change in her outlook and her language.

The common thing here is that, while these women had good friends that they could have great conversations with, they could see that in their current situation this other need of theirs would not be met – having thought-provoking, stimulating and purposeful discussions around their area of expertise with other people who are also interested in the same topics. In a conversation with a woman who had done one of my 'Empowered Women: From Retired to Redefined' courses, she described the whole experience of participating as providing her a link with aspects of her working life that she missed. Being able to use her skills, contributing her unique perspective, collaborating, focusing on a key objective and being part of a shared outcome was the golden thread that linked the work that she does in the group created by attending the course, and her old life of work.

There is also the desire to still feel relevant. One of the things that the women hated the most about stopping work was the assumption that others made about the fact that they would no longer be able to contribute to society, and that they would be perceived as being irrelevant.

It's definitely worth thinking ahead to determine what you might need to do to ensure that the things that matter to you in a work environment – that energize you and keep you young – are still in your life. Maybe one of the ways of doing this is to think about what contributes to your work persona and your work skillset that you can use and draw on when no longer at work.

If having stimulating, challenging discussions is important, where will your new forum for this be? Do you need to think about setting something up, or do you need to think about what you can access in a different way? Just because you're no longer working in that field, does that mean that you no longer have anything to contribute? How can you think about things in a different way, so that you can find forums where your experience and knowledge are an asset, and will be considered as a valuable contribution to any discussions? Finding ways to be involved in ongoing conversation and debate concerned with your subject area could provide you with exactly what you're looking for. Some people find this through completely different forums and become part of a new community. This sense of being part of something larger, and the idea of contributing your knowledge and experience to the benefit of others, is a key ingredient of *ikigai*, a concept and way of living that is important in Japan, which I will explore further in Chapter 10 (see p. 120). There is a strong association between this element of *ikigai* and enjoying a long, satisfying and fruitful life – so it's definitely something to take seriously.

What can you learn from…

Dominique

Dominique was someone who had had a variety of roles and had always learnt new things because of this. Having worked long hours for many years, she was relishing not being at her desk for eight hours every day (and seeing the benefits in how her body felt), but took some time to realize that she needed to work out what she needed to add into her life now she was no longer at work. She described her first winter after retiring, and that all she was doing was learning a new language in a 'desultory fashion'. This was a low time for her, and she thought: 'I have to do something.'

She decided to take things in hand and experiment. She now goes to art classes which she has found interesting, she is taking a course in a subject that she already knows a lot about, and she's studying new things – which she's keen to do even more of. For her, this range of activities is stimulating and keeps her curious, interested and interesting.

Annabel

Having worked for many years in a demanding role and combining this with being a mother and caring for her elderly parents, Annabel thought about all the things she had wanted to do but hadn't been able to because she hadn't had the time. She was incredibly positive about life after work, and one of the things she is doing for the first time is an art class. She described herself as having 'created this new hobby'.

Mia

Having had a highly specialized job, and working in a very long-hours culture, Mia's need to continue to keep up to date in her area of speciality, and to stimulate her brain by learning new things, was very high. In order to keep current, she decided to remain as a member of the organizations that would provide her with the latest information and discussion. This was because of her own interest, but also because there could be the possibility that her knowledge and experience might be called upon in a consultancy role for short-term projects. She also decided to apply for a voluntary post for which she would need to learn a significant amount about a completely new area, and that would also require continual learning once she was in post. She has struck a balance between being in control of her time and having the flexibility to do what she wants during the majority of her days, and working in this new role which is stimulating and new.

> ## Step 3 of your journey
>
> Complete the following exercises in as much or as little detail as is right for you – remember this is for you, and might only be read by you. It will, however, form part of your design for your future. If you would find it easier to talk through your answers rather than writing or drawing them, you could choose a trusted person to work with, or even dictate your answers into a device (for example your phone).

Spend some time thinking about the following questions, so that you're clearer about what you might want to learn and why:

1. Do you want to learn something new because:
   a) you want to meet others?
   b) you have a goal?
   c) you're interested in that particular topic?

2. Thinking about other times when you have learnt something new:
   a) What has been your motivation?
   b) What was the outcome?
   c) What was the best thing for you about the experience?

3. Thinking about learning, what makes your heart sing? Why?*

4. If you were to throw all caution to the wind and be really brave, what would you decide to do?

*You will be adding this to your map at the end of the book.

8: Your travelling companions (relationships)

We are communal animals. We need each other.
Gloria Steinem

'NO (WO)MAN IS an island' is an old adage – and for good reason, as acknowledged by Gloria Steinem in an interview for BBC's *Woman's Hour* in April 2024.[1] In all communities around the world the common way of living is in groups, and we know from current research that, as well as making people happier, there is a direct link between not being with people – and therefore being lonely – and physical and mental health. One of the things that typifies the Blue Zones around the world (the areas where there are the highest numbers of people living over the age of 100) is that they all have strong communities.[2] People come together every day to share food, laughter and ideas, or to exercise and talk. We also know from Gratton and Scott's findings in *The 100-Year Life*[3] (see p. 7) that it is important to be in contact with a variety of different people, and spending more time with family and friends was a common theme among the women I spoke to when writing this book.

This chapter will look at the benefits of different types of relationships.

We are social beings

As humans we are herd animals and live and function optimally within groups – family groups, groups in the community, educational groups, work groups and social groups. In fact, our need to be part of a wider group can be a life-or-death matter. Research into babies in institutional settings who had been well cared for in a practical sense – fed and kept clean – but neglected in terms of having been spoken to and held (in other words, not had what we think of as 'human contact') shows that the death rate was much higher than for other babies who had had both practical care and human contact.[4] While the worry had been that these babies might contract diseases from the contact and then die, they actually died at higher rates simply because they were not nurtured by contact.

Our need to be in regular contact with other people at all stages of our lives is an important factor to consider when approaching the stage of no longer working. And having different types of connections is also important. Having diverse networks is one of the main intangible asserts that Gratton and Scott focus on in *The 100-Year Life*, and it's important to invest time and effort in this at different stages of our lives. The more diverse our network – made up of friends, family, colleagues, people with shared interests, people with different interests and from different backgrounds – the better.

A couple of women I spoke to had found that they had recently gained an immeasurable amount by joining a cause – either a campaigning group, or a group dedicated to learning and creating together. This had meant that they had spent time with people of all different ages and from different walks of life, who had joined together with the same aim or passion, thus building a 'community of achievement'. This had a significant impact on them and their outlook.

It might be that we have many friends at work, or that, while our colleagues are not part of our friendship circle, we still appreciate the contact we have with them – the opportunity to share ideas, perspectives, reactions and experiences. Various studies from across the world show that there are links between loneliness and both physical and mental health. For example, being lonely can impact on sleep, cardiovascular disease and diabetes, and reducing loneliness can be important in warding off dementia.[5] Having lots of positive social relationships is associated with being a 'superager' (someone whose memory skills are those of someone much younger) and, conversely, having few social interactions has been shown to be linked to an increased risk in dementia.[6] Reducing loneliness is one of the top five things that Andrew Steptoe of the English

Longitudinal Study of Ageing highlights as of importance to having a good life after work.[7]

Who do you need, and why?

Colleagues

Stopping work can have both a negative and a positive impact on how you view your social network. On the one hand, people are aware that they will miss their colleagues, the daily interaction with people connected with work (rather than friends outside work), and the stimulation that comes with exchanging ideas. The fact that you don't have any choice about whether or not you interact with someone you might not normally choose to can lead to frustration, but also to appreciating perspectives that are different from your own. The relationships with people at work sit outside the social norm of choosing to be with people because you like them, and who are often similar to you in outlook, upbringing and worldview. Instead, they are based around what you need to achieve together – they have the structure of work outcomes to hold them together. This sense of collaboration and mutual endeavour is one of the main benefits cited by women doing my 'Empowered Women: From Retired to Redefined' courses. While they each bring their own specific set of experiences and challenges, the whole group works with them to help to clarify the situation and suggest ways forward for them.

Another aspect you might miss about your work colleagues is that you like them and enjoy spending time with them, both at work and outside work. Or it could be that your colleagues know a very different side to you from anyone outside work – they can see your value to the organization and know your strengths, skills and vulnerabilities that show up in a work situation. It could be beneficial to you right now to consider who will be able to replace what your work colleagues provide for you once you're no longer at work.

Whatever your experience, many people they will miss this 'enforced' daily interaction with people once they stop working, so it could be useful to work out who you might want to continue seeing, and how often. Or it could be that you and a group of your colleagues would benefit from getting together regularly, so that you can re-live your work experiences – sharing the highs, the lows and the laughs.

In my conversations with several of the women I spoke to, it was interesting how many of them said that leaving the social environment of work for a situation where they won't see people every day, would have been much more difficult to do if it hadn't been for the COVID-19 pandemic. For those not working on the front line, they suddenly found themselves in the situation of not being with colleagues every day. While they still had meetings (online), so spoke to each other, these meetings were much more process-driven – gone were the 'water cooler' moments, the downtime at the office, and other opportunities to have more social conversations. Whether they had already left work, or were planning to do so, these women acknowledged that things would have been different if they had been making this change prior to March 2020, and it will be interesting to see what the impact of hybrid working might be on people in the future when they stop working – on how much they will miss their work colleagues.

When I read about the meaning of work, and how this might impact on the decisions people make about what to do when they have stopped working, I was interested to see that social meaning was cited; the others were personal (connected to growth and development), financial, and generative (sharing experiences and knowledge).[8] The social meaning that people attach to work feeds into their sense of belonging and, if people find that as they get older they experience social loss, they are more likely to seek out post-retirement employment. This absolutely makes sense if one of the most important components of work is being with others.

Friends

Many of the women I spoke to were looking forward to spending more time with friends and family once they stopped work. Some were aware of friendships that they had let slip over the years due to a lack of time, and were interested in re-igniting these relationships. Others very much considered that some people were in your lives for certain periods and then gradually drifted out of your lives, which they considered to be a normal pattern in life. It's interesting that Gratton and Scott, in *The 100-Year Life*, name 'regenerative friendships' as one of the key 'intangible assets' – or the things that we should all invest in throughout our lives in order to have a meaningful longer life. They highlight the benefits of nurturing these regenerative friendships – the ones with people you have known for a very long time, who have seen you change and develop, and who have known your joys and your challenges.

Whether or not the friendships were old ones or new ones, the emphasis on being able to enjoy spending more time with friends when work was no longer a focus came up again and again among the women I spoke to. The importance of investing in these friendships, and spending time with people who are important to them and understand and know them, was clear. There was also a drive to meet new people and make new friends. Someone I spoke to who moved location when she stopped working said that her existing friends warned her against doing this, as she wouldn't know anyone. Instead, she met new people who she became friendly with, and now spends time with both sets of friends. It's almost as if, without the structure of work filling the days, there is the realization that human contact, and the fun, stimulation and depth of conversation that can come with that, is of very great importance. Attendees of my courses have highlighted how they want to expand their network of friends, to have more fun and laughter, to have more meaningful relationships, and it can be useful to think about how you can do this. They have found that doing my course is one of the ways they have been introduced to a group of new people, and are positive about the way these friendships will continue to develop over time.

What do you need to access, how do you need to think and behave differently, and where do you need to go so that you're meeting more people, and a wider range of people? As different people we interact with bring out different aspects of our character, seeing a wide variety of people is key. As one woman said: 'I believe in relationships – they're absolutely essential to what we do.'

Family

Not being at work anymore means that there is a lot more time that can be spent with family members – both for pleasure, and, at times, out of necessity. And this necessity could apply to caring for grandchildren and caring for parents. Sweden, which was the first country to introduce paid paternity leave over 50 years ago (in 1974), has recognized the important role that many grandparents play when it comes to childcare by introducing a law in which parents can now transfer up to 45 days of their paid parental leave to grandparents or friends.

With the cost of childcare in the UK so high, and with the tendency for parents to be working at least part-time, many people who stop working find themselves in the situation of looking after grandchildren on a regular basis. This could be something that they choose, or something that they feel they need to do – a way of supporting their adult children, and a way to feel that they can get to know their grandchildren well and be involved with them at a young age. I often hear women talk about how different being a grandparent is compared to being a parent; you have more experience and, because you're not with the children all the time, your relationship with them can be a very special one. I also hear women saying that they feel they don't have a choice other than to help out, and that it can feel more of a duty.

With the gradual increase in life expectancy (see Chapter 4) many people who stop working then spend time caring for their parents and, for some of the women I interviewed, this was a contributory factor to their decision to stop, and something they felt glad to be able to do. Being able to put boundaries round this role, however, can prove to be challenging, as when you have lots more time on your hands it can be expected that you will spend more of it than you may want to in this caring role. For both these caring roles, it's important to work out what you're happy to do, and then be very clear about this to those around you, so that you don't feel resentful that you've lost a lot of the precious time that you have gained by stopping work.

For the women I spoke to who were choosing to spend time with their family on a more informal basis, the happiness about this really shone through. I heard again and again how much they enjoyed spending time with their adult children, and the joy they took in being with their grandchildren – particularly if they had had very little time to do this when they were working: 'I wanted, for once, to say "I can hang out with the grandchildren". It's been really good.'

Partner

If you have a partner, the time when you've stopped working can be wonderful – an opportunity for you to spend time together doing lots of things you've always wanted to do but haven't had the time for. Or it can be challenging, with you both adjusting to everything that not being at work means to you, and to spending a lot more time together. It's interesting that, while divorce rates in the UK are on the decrease, there is an upward trend in divorce among the over 50s – it even has the title 'grey divorce', with divorcees called 'silver splitters'.[9] The increase in divorce in this demographic has doubled since 1990, and is expected to triple by 2030, and between 2005 and 2015 the number of women who got divorced over the age of 65 rose by 38%. While finances and empty nest syndrome are cited as key reasons for divorce at this time, so is retirement. This could be because couples have gradually grown apart, or because they have both been working and focusing on raising children, so have had a shared purpose. Now that these adult children have moved out, this shared purpose isn't there anymore. The idea of being an older divorcee is also much more possible than in the past, because many women now are more financially independent than women from previous generations. Putting all these things together, and then adding to the mix the idea that we all might live for a lot longer (maybe even up to 30 years after leaving work), it's understandable why many couples might think that their relationship is no longer viable or enjoyable. Someone I was talking to recently mentioned a friend who is spending a lot longer at the gym now that her husband is retired; we wondered if it's because she needs to have a reason to spend more time away from him!

Even for the majority of couples who decide to stay together, adjusting to a change in life – apart and together – that this stage of their relationship brings, can be tricky. The two people in the relationship could have very different needs in terms of what makes them feel happy, fulfilled and content, and one of them could adjust to life after work much more easily than the other. Realizing that there could be the possibility of spending a lot of time of every day together – or finding that you're 'answerable' to someone else when planning your day-to-day life – could put a real strain on the relationship.

Someone I spoke to about this anticipated that she and her partner would need to think about how much time they might want to spend together, and how much apart, and that they would both need to work out and discuss what they expected of each other. Someone else said that she had anticipated that she and her husband would do a lot more together, but had now changed to thinking that they needed to have more time apart doing separate things. Another woman said that she and her partner did a few things together, but they were mostly involved in different activities. As she said: 'That's important, because we come together in the evening and have things to tell each other and talk about.'

Being proactive and talking about this as a couple so that you're honest and are each aware of the other's needs, could be a really good idea.

As well as the realm of everyday living together, there is also the wider picture of what either of you want for the next chunk of your lives – and whether or not these wishes match up. It's interesting to hear how many people don't actually have the sort of honest and sometimes difficult conversations that are necessary at times of significant life changes, but if you both make assumptions about what the other person wants and needs depending on your own desires, then trouble could be afoot. If you share the same values, and know that the same big things are important to you both, then it's easier to find a way through the other stuff.

What can you learn from…

Annie

Annie is a woman I spoke to who was fizzing with energy, ideas and passion. Passion for the creative work she did, passion for campaigning (she had championed women all her professional life and was a leader in her profession), and passion for being with lots of different groups of people. She believes that one of the most important things you can do throughout your life – and particularly when you're older and are not meeting so many people through work – is to participate in lots of different types of activities. Not only do you then develop your interests, learn new things and deepen your knowledge or skills, you meet new people, and it is this meeting of new people that she believes is especially beneficial. Through this you have your thinking challenged, you get to hear other perspectives, and you keep curious. In particular, she talked about participating in craft activities, which tend to be very popular with younger people in their 30s, as well as older people. This bringing together of people of different ages to do the same activity, where the focus is working with your hands on something of beauty, means that conversation happens in a different way to when there isn't this creative focus. When I asked her what her biggest piece of advice would be for people stopping work, she said: 'Don't let go of your connections, they make you feel alive, vital, interesting, interested, and help to keep your mind active.'

Shannon

Shannon's life has been changed immeasurably by getting involved in an environmental movement that she feels very strongly about and meeting a wide range of different people who share this same passion. Working together for a common cause, hearing their stories and their life experiences has had a huge impact on her and her outlook. As well as her involvement with that national organization, she is now taking part in local campaigns, using the skills of mediating and negotiating that she had gained throughout her career. This campaigning is also bringing her into contact with other local people that she hadn't previously met, expanding her circle of friends. Her sense of belonging to the place she has recently moved to is deepening through this work and these connections.

Step 4 of your journey

Complete the following exercises in as much or as little detail as is right for you – remember this is for you, and might only be read by you. It will, however, form part of your design for your future. If you would find it easier to talk through your answers rather than writing or drawing them, you could choose a trusted person to work with, or even dictate your answers into a device (for example your phone).

1. Thinking of the people you know, who gives you energy, and who drains your energy? It

could be useful to focus on those that give you energy.

2. Thinking about your friends, what is it you recognize in your relationships with each one that you benefit from? Is there anything missing? If so, where/who are you going to get this from?

3. If you have a partner, think about spending time together and spending time apart. How much time for each do you want or need? What about your partner – what do you think they want or need?

4. Draw a big circle with you in the middle of it. Draw in other important people and think about the significance of where you have placed them, and which direction they are facing.*

*You will be adding this to your map at the end of the book.

9: Your travelling gear (identity, image and status)

Question: 'How much is your view of yourself tied up in your status at work?'

Answer: 'A lot! It's a large part of my identity!'

Perceptions of age

IN MY READING around the subject of stopping work and ageing, I have come across the word 'juvenescence' – the concept of staying younger for longer.[1] This links in with the whole discourse about longevity, and the fact that, since 1841, there has been a gradual increase in life expectancy. In the UK in 2011, life expectancy at birth was almost double what it had been in 1841, and by 2025, 50% of the UK population will be over the age of 50.[2]

The concept of juvenescence brings into focus the whole new way of thinking about age, and is completely counter to the image of a retiree who spends the majority of their day being sedentary and of thinking of this time as their 'twilight years'.

The post-menopausal you

As mentioned earlier in the book, much has been written recently about the symptoms of menopause, and menopause training in the workplace is becoming more accepted. It is right and proper that there is a much greater level of understanding of the physical, psychological and emotional changes that women can go through during the menopause. What there seems to be less of, though, is information about the way women are once they are post-menopausal. The changes in hormones that happen during the menopause – including the decline in oestrogen – mean that the brain's structure alters, which can affect mood.[3] After the menopause, however, there is a stabilization of the brain. In fact, in traditional Chinese herbal medicine, the years after menopause are thought of as a time of 'rebirth'.[4]

So, what do you want the reborn you to look like? So many of the women I have talked to really do consider these years to be ones of liberation. They're not at the mercy of fluctuating hormones, they tend to care less about what other people think, and really invest their time and energy in what they really want to do and what they feel strongly about – and there's less pressure to be sexually attractive. In Ruth Ray Karpen's article on women retiring in the journal *The Gerontologist,* she asserts that women look for new outlets for their skills, and that there can be a shift in their attitude toward work – going from work they need to do, to work they want to do.[5] Thinking again about women's career development theory, it could be that if women haven't managed to carve out an 'authentic' stage to their career, they might well do that when they stop working – or when they go on to do other work once they have officially retired.

Your view versus society's view

In conversation with lots of women my age, feeling much younger internally than they actually are, is a very common topic. Often women feel some age between 25 and 45, despite being 55 or 65 or 75! How often do you see an older woman walking toward you when you're in a shopping street, only to quickly realize that you are actually looking at yourself in a mirror? This raises the issue that not only does society view older women in a certain (usually negative) way, but also that we don't feel like the older woman that we are. Our real selves are still the same, although our life's experiences will mean that we are different from our younger selves.

This can also be the time when women become grandmothers for the first time, and this involves another identity shift – also with connotations of being old. From my conversations with lots of women, it seems that it is during the time before the first grandchild is born that some women struggle with a new identity that they will be adding to their existing one. I've heard people say things like, 'I don't feel old enough to be a grandmother', and 'It's making me feel a lot older', and 'I don't feel ready for this next life stage'. It's another time of life that people tend to make assumptions about; they expect the older woman to feel delighted and excited, and it is rarely acknowledged that these feelings could be mixed with doubt and uncertainty about their own identity, how they view themselves, and how they think others will view them.

We live in an era where ageism is rife – so much so that in 2021 top female entrepreneur Lindsey Simpson set up 55/Redefined as an organization which describes itself as 'the UK's consumer champion for the over-50s' – and it can be difficult to convey who our real selves are. Add being a woman into the mix and we can see that gendered ageism doesn't just exist in the workplace, but in the whole of society – and one of the impacts of this is on healthcare practices. This is highlighted in a 2021 article in *The Lancet*,[6] and was also echoed by the women I spoke to – one of whom had worked in a male-dominated environment for over 25 years, but felt completely ignored, and her opinion dismissed, when seeking specialist information about a health condition.

Another point raised by this article in *The Lancet* is the effect of ageism on how visible older women are. This has been reinforced time and time again by the women I have spoken to. One said that she remembers her own mother saying that people aren't listened to in the same way once they get older, and another one – an experienced teacher – feels invisible and 'silenced' by her adult children and their partners. For them, her knowledge and experience count for nothing – they think that the world has moved on. They are not acknowledging or valuing her wisdom and sagacity; this is in contrast to the attitude toward older people in many Eastern societies, who are revered and seen as being wise.

We also see gendered ageism in how women present themselves, feeling pressure not to reveal their age, or dyeing their hair so that it doesn't look white, for example. Older men are often referred to as 'silver foxes' – where is the equivalent description of women with white hair?

Identity and image

Something that emerged in my interviews and conversations was the link between people's identity and work, how they described themselves once they'd stopped working, and whether or not status was important to them. Wherever you sit on the spectrum between all these things mattering a lot to you and them not mattering at all, it could be useful to unpick this a bit for yourself.

One definition of identity focuses on the social interaction between self and society, and, of course, 'society' could mean different things to different people, or could include a variety of interactions. If, for example, someone's self-identity is strongly tied to work, the more they might struggle when they are no longer at work (and the more likely they are to look for paid employment in retirement). Taking a bit of time to think about how this might apply to you could be enlightening, and could give you ideas for reducing any potential challenge when you leave work. For instance, if you think that your identity is related to your work, it might well be that you want to take on some sort of work role (albeit in a different form) in the future. You might want to work in a more ad hoc way on a consultancy or mentoring basis in the area that you know a lot about, or you might want a complete change in work arena. If, however, someone's self-identity is strongly rooted in their relationships to others (a wife, a partner, a daughter, a mother, a sister, for example) the more likely they are to focus on this once they no longer work.

When I asked my interviewees who had stopped working how they describe themselves now, their replies ranged from 'retired', to 'a retired banker' to 'a banker', which clearly demonstrated to me how much their work title meant to them in terms of their sense of identity. Only a couple of the people I asked were happy with the term 'retired' to describe themselves and their life stage. The vast majority of the others didn't like the negative connotations that come with the word – of giving the impression of being irrelevant, of being 'past it', of being perceived as a drain on society. They either couldn't think of another word, or used a phrase to describe themselves and this stage. Here are some of their ideas:

> I'm having a gap year.
>
> I've stopped work/I've given up work.
>
> I'm not working, but I'm doing things that are different.
>
> I'm just going into the next phase of my life.
>
> I took an opportunity during restructuring to do what I want to do.
>
> I'm retired and I do a mixture of things.

Haven't got a clue. I really don't know.

Conjures up someone who's old (older than me) who probably doesn't do a great deal.

One of the inspiring things about listening to these women describe their current life stage, was the positivity, gratitude and joyousness they expressed, including:

The art of the possible.

It's about opportunities.

It's a time of regeneration

It's a precious time of your life if you're lucky enough to have enough money and good health.

It's a golden age really. I choose to do these things. It's a lovely stage of my life.

How can you change the narrative and tell a new story?

These descriptions are in strong contrast to society's view of people who are retired, or of pensionable age, and it could be different from how we might have viewed our parents at this age. In a recent conversation with a woman about her female friends who were stopping work, she used words such as 'powerful', 'full of energy', 'strong', 'inspiring' – not words traditionally associated with retirement, and definitely not associated with the image of sitting around and relaxing for the majority of the time. If women feel more powerful when they have gone through the menopause, why would this feeling go away, and why are we not recognizing it as a society? Where is the new vocabulary to describe this life stage?

So how do you navigate your way between these two different images – your image of yourself and this life stage (your energy, what you want to achieve, how young you might feel inside), and the image that others might have of you? How much do you find that your thinking and your vocabulary are affected by your age, and how could you change this if you wanted to? Who do you need to surround yourself with so that you feel both that you're with others who understand and appreciate you, and also that you keep young in thinking and perspective? As mentioned in Chapter 7, a few of the women that I have spoken to have highlighted that one of the things they really miss about work is being with people a lot younger than themselves. They loved hearing about new trends, new ways of thinking, new music, new fashion, and really appreciated being presented with the different perspectives brought by their younger colleagues. Becoming a mentor to younger women, or a panel expert on training or higher education courses are a couple of different ways of still meeting younger people who can bring fresh ideas and views.

This leads me on to challenge you to think about what story you're currently telling yourself and other people. Is this a story of power, experience and wisdom, or of apology, under-confidence and frailty? If you're not happy with the story you're telling, how can you change it, what do you want to change it to, and who are you going to tell it to? How can you reframe your current position so that it is one of confidence, energy and excitement informed by everything that has gone before? The words you use and particularly the demeanour you give off will make a huge difference to how what you say is received – don't forget that body language and tone account for far more of what is actually 'heard' than words alone.

Is it status you're concerned about?

I asked all the women I interviewed the question: 'How important was status to you in the world of work and how do you feel about status now?'

Having made the assumption that many of them would struggle with this change, I was surprised by the answers I received. Although status was important for some of them, for others, different things were much more significant, such as contributing and feeling valued, making an impact and collaborating. Here are some of the words that the women used:

> Not particularly important but I just wanted to be useful – contributing to something.
>
> It's less about status, it's more about collaboration. Getting respect for what you know and could help to do.

All of these are internal drivers which motivated what the women wanted the outcome of their work to be, and how they wanted to work so that they could be effective. When thinking about status, that's more of an external image – how others perceive you, your ranking compared to others in your environment, and how much emphasis the individual puts on this – and it is recognized that there is a link between the importance of job status and negative effects in early retirement. I found it interesting that lots of the women who had changed the trajectory of their career when they had a family – maybe moving from a full-time high-powered role to a part-time role with less status attached to it – were able to recognize that status had been important to them in their early careers, but that they had gone through a down-shift in their status. They had already adapted to this change and so, for them, the issue of status wasn't a current one.

The fact that it is loss of status – rather than some other internal motivators – that is correlated with experiencing challenges in the early stages of retirement could be because it might be easier to embark on things that have an impact, are valued and are collaborative in the world outside of work, than it is to retain a sense of status. If this is so, then this leads to the question of what ways can you find to be valued by friends and family now? What is it that you can offer that isn't associated with being at work? Ideas about this whole concept form an integral part of Chapter 10.

What can you learn from…

Bernadette

Bernadette has always been someone who likes to be busy and get things done. She said that, for her, status in itself wasn't important, but ambition was. She wanted to get to the top of her field (which she did) so that she could be in charge and be effective. As she said: 'Men feel valued for their opinion, women feel valued for what they can do.'

She stepped down from this role about ten years before she stopped working as she couldn't get the flexibility she wanted, and went on to set up her own business working in her area of expertise. Because she could adapt the hours she worked to other things going on in her life, and also because she worked on interesting projects, she felt like she had been 'sort of in transition for ten years'.

At this point she also had voluntary roles that were important to her; she was a trustee of a big choir, a school governor and the chair of the board at a local hospice, so the adjustment to leaving the workforce wasn't a big one for her. She is someone who likes to do a lot of different things and wants to be in a position to make things happen, and this is in alignment with how she was at work. She still refers to her former profession when asked what she does, so although her motivator at work was to get to the top in order to get things done, she is still very tied to her professional title.

Nora

Having left her full-time role several years ago, Nora still identifies herself by the work she does, and this is an intrinsic part of her identity. She told me early on in our conversation: 'I am defined by my work.'

She has no intention of stopping work; she has always loved the world of work, and is very clear that it has given her sense of identity. When she talks about herself now, she uses her current work title, and I get the sense that this will change when she stops her current role and moves on to the next thing. Her identity is so inextricably linked to the work she does, that she can't imagine what she will call herself if she should ever not be involved in something that she views as work. The moving on to the next thing that interests, excites and energizes her is her driving force, which means she's open to new ideas and opportunities. She knows herself well enough to know that this is a need of hers.

Step 5 of your journey

Complete the following exercises in as much or as little detail as is right for you – remember this is for you, and might only be read by you. It will, however, form part of your design for your future. If you would find it easier to talk through your answers rather than writing or drawing them, you could choose a trusted person to work with, or even dictate your answers into a device (for example your phone).

Identity
1. How will you describe yourself once you have stopped working?

    Try drawing an image of yourself (it could be as simple as a stick person) and label it, to help with your description.

2. Think about what image you want to convey to others, how you want to be perceived, how you want to feel about yourself. Try practising saying it to yourself to see how it 'fits' you.

3. What phrase will you use that will encapsulate this next stage of your life? You might never need to say this to anyone, but it's a great idea to at least think it!

4. Put together your description of yourself, and of this next phase of your life.*

Image

Draw up a list of words that bring up the image for you of someone who is old, and think of an alternative; I've made suggestions for the first couple.

Commonly used words	Your alternative
Old	Elder
Past it	Experienced

Think about how often you use the words in the left-hand column, and start instead to introduce the words in the right-hand column.

> **Your motivator at work**
>
> Write down what you think motivated you at work – was it status, adding value, feeling valued, collaborating, etc.?
>
> Keep this in mind for the work you do in Chapter 10.
>
> * You will be adding this to your map at the end of the book.

10: Your compass (meaning and purpose)

I'm not working, but I'm doing things that are different. The art of the possible.

THERE CAN BE a sense of luxury about having lots of time stretching ahead, but it can also bring a feeling of panic to some people. They might think, 'How am I going to fill that time?', or 'What am I "allowed" to do with all this time?', or 'Should I be doing something more with my time?'. This sense of 'filling time' can be viewed in different ways. If you have had many years of being very busy at work, you might need to have this feeling of ever-expanding time, of being able to make daily decisions dependent on the weather or how you're feeling, of taking a long time over breakfast or lunch, of catching up with friends and family. It could be that you realize that while you have this approach for a while, this could change, and in the future you might want to fill your time with something more. Or it could be that you need to have something that gives you a feeling of purpose as soon as you stop working. In an article in *The Guardian* in December 2023 writer, director and theatre producer Carol Allen (aged 82) said: 'Work, for me, is purpose. Without work – that is to say, without staying part of society – my life would be without purpose.'[1]

What is *ikigai*, and what is your *ikigai*?

I became interested in the concept of *ikigai* when watching the documentary *Blue Zones*.[2] These Blue Zones are areas in the world where there are communities that have an unusually high number of centenarians. Author and journalist Dan Buettner visited these communities and talked to the older group members to find out about them and their lifestyle, and to try to discover if there were aspects to their lives that were common across all the communities. One of the communities was in Okinawa, a Japanese island in the East China Sea between mainland Japan and Taiwan, and, in conversation with the elders in this community, the concept of *ikigai* was discussed. The word *ikigai* can be roughly translated as 'the happiness of always being busy', but it's not just about busyness, it's about combining your skills and things that you love to do, and contributing in some way to your community or the world. For people who have found their *ikigai*, they have meaning and purpose to every day – and the great thing is that no one's *ikigai* is the same as anyone else's, and, if you haven't found your meaning and purpose yet, using your curiosity and your intuition can be an effective approach.

You will already know what your skills are – you will have been using them all your life, both at work and outside of work, and you will have been gathering more and more of them during your life's course. What can be harder to do is working out what you love to do, combining this with your skills, and also contributing in some way to life outside yourself. Listening to what the women say who have done my courses, I wonder if their participation provides them with *ikigai* when they are working together. They are certainly bringing their skills and experience and contributing to the group (that is, to something outside of themselves).

There seems to be a strong link between being an artist – feeling compelled to create – and *ikigai*, which is probably why so many people who are creative continue to create things for the whole of their lives. Think back to the mother of one of the women I spoke to who, at the age of 93, is still painting every day. The daughter (in her 60s) is firmly of the belief that everyone is creative, but not everyone has discovered what they are creative at – yet!

There is also a link between *ikigai* and the state of 'flow'. This is when you immerse yourself completely in something; you're not distracted, you lose all sense of time, and you're completely focused on what you're doing. Being in flow is thought of as the optimal way to be, and it usually involves building on a skill, and doing something that you love. There is usually some kind of challenge involved – it's not about maintaining the status quo.

To uncover what has meaning for you – what a 'meaningful' task is – you first need to be sure that you know what your own personal values are, as these need to be aligned to the tasks (see the exercise at the end of this chapter).

The feeling of the need for meaning and purpose was expressed time and again in my conversations with women. One of them said: 'It's a mental thing – being without purpose. How do you survive?' Another said: 'I'm trying to fill my time with things that I feel are worth something.'

This is completely in tune with what García and Miralles state in their book about *ikigai*: 'If you want to stay busy even when there's no need to work, there has to be an ikigai on the horizon, a purpose that guides you throughout your life and pushes you to make things of beauty and utility for the community and for yourself.'[3]

One of the women expressed the quest for something that has meaning and purpose in terms of her future self, saying: 'How will I feel at 80, looking back over the years – have I done enough?'

However people express it, and whatever they need in order to fulfil it, there's no doubt that doing something with meaning and purpose is linked to having a happy (and hopefully healthy) longer life. A big study of 7,000 people over the age of 50 conducted by the University of Michigan School of Public Health, found that there was a link between purpose and longevity – and that having purpose was more positively correlated with decreased mortality than gender, race or education.[4]

Hobbies or new work?

It may be easier to find your *ikigai* if you're one of those people who does things that they love in their spare time, who feels passionately about their hobbies. But what if you don't have any hobbies? You can't just invent them – suddenly decide you're really interested in something and want to spend a lot of time dedicated to it, to improving at it, to finding out more. The pressure that the word 'hobby' brings can feel overwhelming and lead to a sense of failure, or that you're lacking in some way.

If we relate this to the concept of *ikigai*, it could be that it's more about finding your new 'work': doing something that uses your skills and aptitudes, that you enjoy and think is important, and that includes a feeling of 'giving back'. This phrase of 'giving back' was frequently used by the women I spoke to – they felt that having left their professions, they now had the time to take the opportunity to do something for others. This might be in the form of volunteering, or mentoring; of being a non-executive director, or of helping out in a care home; of being involved in looking after grandchildren, or being an expert on a panel. Whatever it is that people choose to do, it needs to be right for them – and not necessarily someone else's suggestion.

Several of the women I spoke to had discovered great joy and a sense of purpose from finding a voluntary role that really suited their skillset and passion. For two of them, it involved cooking – one with asylum seekers and the other with underprivileged families. For one of them it was gardening (she had previously trained in horticulture), and for another it was being on the board of her local hospice. As one of these women said, she believes that people should volunteer, 'but you've actually got to find what pleases you. I'm using my skills doing what I enjoy'.

Going on to paid work

It could be that you want to go on to having more paid work, maybe with differences in time, responsibility and stress to your previous role, and we know that there is a link between how people view work (the meaning it has for them) and whether or not they are more likely to look for paid work once they retire. Or it could be that you don't have the option of not having any paid work anymore. With the rise in life expectancy, the subsequent increase in the number of years that you might live post-retirement, and the declining value of pensions, needing to earn money until an older age could be an imperative. In their book *The 100-Year Life*,[5] Gratton and Scott promote the virtues of a 'portfolio career' – one in which people are moving on to other things at different stages, or are combining a variety of roles at the same time. Indeed, this is one of the 'intangible assets' that they recommend people invest time and energy in preparing for, making sure they are open to new ideas, training and opportunities throughout their working lives. You might not, however, want to do anything that could be viewed as a 'career', but want something that is predictable, has very little stress, brings you in contact with other people, and provides structure to your week. Since 2014, there has been a steady rise in the numbers of people in the UK over the age of 65 who are in employment, many of whom work part-time.[6]

There has also been a big increase in the number of women who have left their paid roles and become entrepreneurs – setting up their own businesses with a focus on following their passions. In fact, looking at the data of people who are actively working above the age of 60 across the whole of the UK population, there is an increasing number of people who are self-employed as they become older.

Career Anchors

The career theorist Edgar Schein devised a theory called Career Anchors.[7] He noticed that people identified more or less strongly with the eight 'constructs' that he described, and this decision was based on the combination of talents, motives and values that the individual recognized in themself. Once someone has worked out what is most important to them, they can use this to help them when they make changes in their career. Simply put, these eight Career Anchors are as follows:

1. *Technical/functional competence*: These people will be good at specific tasks, and it will be important for them to develop the necessary skills for these tasks.
2. *General management competence*: These people like to have positions of responsibility. They are good with high-level problems, at building relationships, and are emotionally intelligent.
3. *Autonomy/independence*: These people do well when left to get on with things themselves without input or direction from others.
4. *Security/stability*: These people want things to be stable and predictable. They often spend a long time in the same position.
5. *Entrepreneurial creativity*: These are the creatives, the inventors. They work well with others and tend to get bored easily and want to move on to the next thing. They often start their own business.

6. *Service/dedication to a cause*: These people find opportunities to help others. They often work in HR.
7. *Pure challenge*: These people are stimulated by new challenges and tasks and will move jobs so that they always have new challenges.
8. *Lifestyle*: These people integrate life and work, and they focus on how their life looks as a whole.

Using this model when preparing for stopping work so that you can decide what is important for you to have in your next life stage, could make a difference to you. You will still have the same talents and skills that you always have had, but your values and motives might well have shifted from when you were focusing on your career. It could be that, for the first time, you decide that helping others is something that has become much more important to you, and this could guide your thinking about what you want to incorporate in your life going forward. Or it could be more a matter of shifting how you use your Career Anchor in a different way. For example, if Technical/functional competence has always been important to you, you might want to think about what task (and then necessary skills) you want to spend time on. Or if you have always liked being involved in things at a high level, enjoying responsibility and fostering good relationships, you might want to look at becoming a trustee of a charity, or joining the board of an organization. Thinking about how you can use what you know about yourself from your working life can help to promote your thinking in a creative way.

As well as thinking about your Career Anchor, it can also help to think about what it is that gives you the most satisfaction and the best feeling of being valued at work. Where can you get this from once you leave work? If, for example, you feel valued when your opinion and expertise are asked for, what forums can you access where this can happen in the future? If you feel valued as part of a team, in what way can you work collaboratively with others in the future?

What can you learn from…

Agathe

When I asked Agathe what had made her feel valued at work, she said it was others coming to her for advice – for her wisdom and experience. Having stopped work a couple of years earlier, she felt a bit directionless and, although she had plenty of things that she could fill her day with, she felt like she needed more: 'I could be busy all the time, but it wouldn't necessarily be the things that give me purpose.'

She had tried volunteering for a national organization, and had done extensive training for this role, but she still didn't have that feeling of purpose and satisfaction. The next time I spoke to Agathe, she told me about a local project that she had got involved in – cooking with asylum seekers. One of her passions is cooking, and she absolutely loved this work. She felt that she was doing something meaningful, that combined her skills and passion for cooking with contributing to a group of people who were in need. When involved in this short-term project, she had found her *ikigai*.

Mia

For the whole of her career, Mia had worked for a national institution which involved her ensuring that she knew her subject in depth, and was in a position to influence and effect positive change. She knew that once she left this job, she would want to continue using her brain, and to continue to make a positive difference to the lives of other people, so she applied to become a magistrate. In this role she was able to use her brilliant and analytical brain with her pragmatic and empathetic approach, in order to give back to society.

Step 6 of your journey

Complete the following exercises in as much or as little detail as is right for you – remember this is for you, and might only be read by you. It will, however, form part of your design for your future. If you would find it easier to talk through your answers rather than writing or drawing them, you could choose a trusted person to work with, or even dictate your answers into a device (for example your phone).

Finding your *ikigai*

Flow:

If you haven't yet found your *ikigai*, there are certain things that could help you to discover it. In their book *Ikigai: The Japanese Secret to a Long and*

Happy Life,[8] Héctor García and Francesc Miralles suggest these stages to help people link their *ikigai* to being in a state of flow:

1. Write down all the activities that help you enter a state of flow.
2. What do these activities have in common?
3. Why do you think these activities drive you to flow?
4. Are the activities just through thinking or doing, or do they also involve movement?

Once you have answered these questions you will have a much better idea of what gets you into a flow state, and you can then choose to do these things more often.

Personal values:
Here are some personal values. Circle the ones that are most important to you; feel free to add more – this isn't an exhaustive list.

Integrity	Generosity	Altruism
Acceptance	Dependability	Authenticity
Family	Adaptability	Assertiveness
Flexibility	Respect	Community
Positivity	Honesty	Loyalty
Self-compassion		

Your skillset:

Think about all aspects of your life (work, relationships, etc.), and write down all of your skills. Then think about what those that work with you, that you are friends with, that know you in any way, would say that your skills are – you could ask them if you like.

Giving back:

So many women that I've spoken to have mentioned wanting to 'give something back' at this stage of their lives. They recognize that they have had the need to work and, now that this is not needed anymore (or not needed in quite the same way), they want to spend some of their time giving back – to society, to their community or to family. What are you involved in, or what do you feel passionately about, that you want to contribute your time to at the moment?

Combine the work you have done on your Career Anchors, what helps you get into a state of flow, what your values are, what your greatest skills are, and in which ways (small or large) you want to contribute – to give something back. This is your *ikigai* at the moment.*

*You will be adding this to your map at the end of the book.

Section 3: Your map – the six-part design for your future

THIS IS WHERE you draw everything together – all your thinking and planning. Just to recap, you need to add your answers to each starred exercise from Chapters 5 to 10 to each section of the template for your design of your map. I have completed the first one with a fictional woman in mind; for those of you growing up in the UK you will understand the reference: this is 'one I have done earlier' in true *Blue Peter* style.[1]

Here are the starred questions from each chapter:

Step 1: My starting point (leaving work)

Draw a mind map to capture your reasons for leaving work:

Get a piece of paper and draw a circle in the middle of it. In this circle write 'My decision to leave'. Draw lines out from this circle, writing a reason at the end of each one. Take note of:

1. how many different reasons there are, and why these matter;
2. which reasons are the most important to you.

Step 2: My timetable (time and structure)

Design your plan for the next week, month and year.

Step 3: My guidebook (learning, growth and connection)

Thinking about learning, what makes your heart sing – and why?

Step 4: My travelling companions (relationships)

Draw a big circle with you in the middle of it. Draw in other important people and think about the significance of where you have placed them, and which direction they are facing.

Step 5: My travelling gear (identity, image and status)

- How will you describe yourself once you have stopped working?

Try drawing an image of yourself (it could be as simple as a stick person) and label it, to help with your description.

- Think about what image you want to convey to others, how you want to be perceived, how you want to feel about yourself. Try practising saying it to yourself to see how it 'fits' you.

- What phrase will you use that will encapsulate this next stage of your life? You might never need to say this to anyone, but it's a great idea to at least think it!

- Put together your description of yourself, and of this next phase of your life.

Step 6: My compass (meaning and purpose)

Combine the work you have done on your Career Anchors, what helps you get into a state of flow, what your values are, what your greatest skills are, and in which ways (small or large) you want to contribute – to give something back. This is your *ikigai* at the moment.

Sara's map (fictional woman)

Step 1:
My starting point (leaving work)

When I drew my mind map, I noticed that there were several different reasons – some practical, some to do with age and lifestyle, and some to do with work itself.

Of all of these, the most important one for me is that I'm not that old, I'm fit and healthy, and I want to make the most of these next few years.

To Step 2

Step 2:
My timetable (change in time and structure)

My plan for:

Week 1:
See friends at least three times.
Do some exercise at least twice.
Go for a walk every day.
Go out in the evening at least twice.
Spend time thinking about what I want to learn/continue learning.
Do some gardening at least twice.

Month 1:
Re-connect with at least two people from the past.
Go away for at least a couple of days.
See a new film or play.
Go to a concert.
Clear out the back bedroom.
Complete my first gardening project.
Research opportunities for me to use my skills and experience in some way.

Year 1:
Expand my network of friends/people I spend time with.
Be fitter.
See real progress in my learning.
Have two long trips away (of at least three weeks each).
Have a plan for my next year.

To Step 3

Step 3:
My guidebook (learning, growth and connection)

When I think about learning, my heart sings when it involves meeting other people from different backgrounds and walks of life, who are interested in the same thing.

Having engaging discussions with them where we talk about our insights.

Finding out more about myself through this process of learning.

To Step 4

Step 4:
My travelling companions (relationships)

The significant people in my circle:

- My husband

I have placed him close to me, and we are facing each other.

- My children

They are further away from me, and are facing to look outside the circle. This is because their lives are all about going forward.

- My sister

She is quite close to me, and is neither facing me nor facing away. We will grow older together and alongside each other.

- Very close friends (six of them)

They are also quite close to me, and neither facing me nor facing away. We will be there for each other, enjoy each other's company, but also live our separate lives.

- Various other friends.

These will move about the circle – in and out, as they are more transient.

To Step 5

Step 5:
My travelling gear (identity, image and status)

My description of myself and of this next phase in my life.

I am someone who is young at heart, but wise. I have had a career working with people and I am still doing some of that work now.

I want to be perceived as someone who is good fun, but that you can also have a decent and deep conversation with.

This next phase of my life is all about getting as much joy from my life as I can, building on doing the things that I love, and being open to new experiences and learning.

It's a time of opportunity!

To Step 6

Step 6:
My compass (meaning and purpose)

What gives me flow?

- gardening
- walking

Common to these:

- being outdoors
- being active

My values:
Integrity, honesty, family, positivity, authenticity, self-compassion

My skills:
Listening, making other people feel at ease, being analytical, empathy

I want to contribute:
Affecting positive change for others by supporting them, helping them to feel part of a community.

Doing things outdoors.

I would like to contribute in the following way:

- Working with others outdoors on a regular basis (weekly). Maybe being involved in wild gardening projects (where they exist).

Your map

(Fill this in with your answers to the key questions from each step of your journey.)

Step 1:
My starting point (leaving work)

To Step 2

Step 2:
My timetable (time and structure)

To Step 3

Step 3:
My guidebook (learning, growth and connection)

To Step 4

Step 4:
My travelling companions (relationships)

To Step 5

Step 5:
My travelling gear (identity, image and status)

To Step 6

Step 6:
My compass (meaning and purpose)

Acknowledgements

There are so many people that I would like to thank that have had an impact on me when writing this book.

First, to my incredibly supportive family and friends: thank you for helping and encouraging me, for giving your ideas, thoughts and opinions, and for taking the time to read and comment on various aspects of the book.

To the many women who I have interviewed or spoken to about this topic: thank you for giving your time, your experience and your insights.

To all of you who have given feedback – on my original ideas, on the various drafts, on the self-reflective exercises: thank you for your input, your perspectives and your encouragement.

To Alison Jones, the team at Practical Inspirations Publishing and to fellow authors: thank you for your support, guidance and wisdom.

About the author

JANE MOFFETT'S WORK and experience over the last 30 years has been women-centred, with a focus on leadership, professional and personal development. Working independently, she has supported women through some of life's major transitions. With pregnancy and childbirth her expertise lies in challenges around the ante-natal period, when first entering motherhood, and on the return to work. She also works with women re-entering work after a career break, as well as with those transitioning out of full-time work into portfolio careers and/or retirement.

She is founder and director of KANGAROO Coaching, working with organizations that are committed to creating progressive workplace cultures. She runs coaching programmes at all organizational levels, from junior employees to C-suite, offering 1:1 and team/group coaching. Her popular 'Empowered Women: From Retired to Redefined' group coaching courses, aimed at late-career stage, are praised for the trust built and the close networks created, as well as the sense of self-development and a greater understanding of the importance of just allowing the process of change to unfold, which comes across so strongly in these words: 'It has given me peace to be me, the most important gift of all!'

Moffett is an Executive Coach, with an MSc in Coaching and Behavioural Change from Henley Business School, and a certified Action Learning Coach. She is a coach assessor and regular contributor to professional coaching journals. Her background in classical music teaching and performance informs her own practice today as a performing and recording member of the Bach Choir.

For further information on Jane Moffett and details on her courses and online materials, go to https://kangaroocoaching.net/from-retired-to-redefined

Resources

The following is a list of some resources that I have found interesting and useful.

Books

Celia Dodd, *Not Fade Away: How to Thrive in Retirement* (Bloomsbury Publishing, 2018).

Héctor García and Francesc Miralles, *Ikigai: The Japanese Secret to a Long and Happy Life* (Hutchinson, 2017).

Lynda Gratton and Andrew J. Scott, *The 100-Year Life: Living and Working in an Age of Longevity* (Bloomsbury, 2020).

Jan Hall and John Stokes, *Changing Gear: Creating the Life You Want After a Full-on Career* (Headline Publishing Group, 2021).

Berit Lewis, *Ageing Upwards: A Mindfulness-Based Framework for the Longevity Revolution* (Practical Inspiration Publishing, 2023).

Lucy Ryan, *Revolting Women: Why Midlife Women Are Walking Out* (Practical Inspiration Publishing, 2023).

Denise Taylor, *Rethinking Retirement for Positive Ageing: Creating a Meaningful Life After Full-time Work* (Routledge, 2024).

Programmes

Live to 100: Secrets of the Blue Zones, created by Dan Buettner, 2023, *Netflix*: www.netflix.com/title/81214929

Podcasts

Emma Thomas, *Middling Along*: https://middling along.com

Sam Baker, *The Shift*: www.youtube.com/playlist?list=PL2aRPnGk7GWYgCemRtLk6pGs2ugQMdE1h

Avivah Wittenberg-Cox, *Life in Four Quarters*: https://howtolive.life/episode/046-life-in-four-quarters-with-avivah-wittenberg-cox

Groups / communities / charities

Noon – organization and community which supports and inspires women who are in their midlife stage: https://noon.org.uk

Restless – digital community for the over-50s: https://restless.co.uk

55/redefined – for the modern over-50 consumer: https://55redefined.co

WB Directors – a purpose-led business working to increase diversity in executive and non-executive leadership, supporting women into non-executive board roles and supporting diverse talent to reach their potential: https://wbdirectors.co.uk

Brilliant Minds – funds early-stage start-ups for the over-50s: https://brilliant-minds.com/

U3A – a UK-wide movement of locally run interest groups where people who are no longer working full-time can come together to learn for fun: www.u3a.org.uk

Reach Volunteering – an organization focused on connecting professionals who want to volunteer, with charities requiring volunteers with specific skills and experience: https://reachvolunteering.org.uk/

Doit Life – government website for volunteers: www.doit.life/volunteer

National Council for Voluntary Organisations – membership organization that champions volunteers and charities: www.ncvo.org.uk

Third Sector – organization which focuses on voluntary sector news and jobs: www.thirdsector.co.uk

Carers UK – charity dedicated to improving the lives of carers: www.carersuk.org/about-us/

Centre for Ageing Better – an organization focused on tackling inequalities in ageing: https://ageing-better.org.uk/

Notes

Introduction

1. Wright, Matt. 'Etymology corner: Retirement – why all retirees should be jubilant', Nobleword, 11 September 2019: www.nobleword.co.uk/etymology-corner-retirement-why-all-retirees-should-be-jubilant/#:~:text=Unsurprisingly%2C%20retirement%20it%20is%20one,tirer"%20(to%20draw)) (accessed 3 October 2024).

2. Gratton, Lynda, and Scott, Andrew J. *The 100-Year Life: Living and Working in an Age of Longevity* (Bloomsbury, 2020).

3. Buettner, Dan. *Live to 100: Secrets of the Blue Zones*, Netflix, 2023: www.netflix.com/title/81214929.

4. Ibarra, Herminia *The Retirement Podcast*, January 2024: www.retirementwisdom.com/podcasts/working-identity-herminia-ibarra/ (accessed 3 December 2024).

Chapter 1

1. Dodwell, Tessa. 'Coaching needs to differ before and after the transition to retirement', *The International Journal of Coaching and Mentoring*, S14, 2020, pp. 102–18.

2. 'The Change Curve': www.exeter.ac.uk/media/university ofexeter/humanresources/documents/learning development/the_change_curve.pdf (accessed 4 October 2024).

3. 'Bridges Model of Transition': https://static1.square space.com/static/5123eb01e4b0b5151b7a8c93/t/5e8ced 28363d81137566744e/1586294057660/Bridges+ Model+of+Transition.pdf (accessed 4 October 2024).

4. Truyens, Marc. 'Transition Theory: Nancy K. Schlossberg 1984', CAREER MARCR for Career Professionals, 2019: https://marcr.net/marcr-for-career-professionals/career-theory/career-theories-and-theorists/transition-theory-nancy-k-schlossberg/ (accessed 4 October 2024).

Chapter 2

1. https://en.wikipedia.org/wiki/Marriage_bar#:~:text= women%20more%20easily.-,History%20in%20the%20 United%20Kingdom,ambivalent%20views%20on%20the %20policy (accessed 7 October 2024).

2. www.ombudsman.org.uk/publications/womens-state-pension-age-our-findings-department-work-and-pensions-communication/background-relating-changes-state-pension-age-women (accessed 7 October 2024).

3. www.legislation.gov.uk/ukpga/1975/65/part/III/cross heading/education/enacted (accessed 7 October 2024).

4. Jones, Jennifer, and Castle, Josephine. 'Women in UK universities, 1920–1980', *Studies in Higher Education*, 11(3), 1986, pp. 289–97.

5. Chandler, Gemma, and Sherida, Leonie. 'Women in work: A brief history of women in the workplace', Lewis Silkin LLP, 2021: www.futureofworkhub.info/comment/2021/7/6/women-in-work-a-brief-history-of-women-in-the-workplace (accessed 11 October 2024).

6. www.ons.gov.uk/peoplepopulationandcommunity/births deathsandmarriages/lifeexpectancies/articles/howhas lifeexpectancychangedovertime/2015-09-09 (accessed 8 October 2024).

7. Chamberlin, Janine. 'Lack of role models hindering women's career progress', HR Director, 2022: www.thehrdirector.com/business-news/diversity-and-equality-inclusion/lack-role-models-hindering-womens-career-progress/ (accessed 8 October 2024).

8. Easton, Mark. 'Women still do more housework survey suggests', BBC News, 21 September 2023: www.bbc.co.uk/news/uk-66866879 (accessed 8 October 2024).

9. 'Women in the workforce: Climbing the ladder and having it all', Propel HR, 2022: www.propelhr.com/blog/women-in-the-workforce-climbing-the-career-ladder-and-having-it-all#:~:text=The%20'80s%20was%20the%20decade, narrowed%20the%20wage%20inequality%20gap (accessed 8 October 2024).

10. 'Women and Pensions', TUC Report, March 2004: www.tuc.org.uk/research-analysis/reports/women-and-pensions#:~:text=In%20fact%2C%20it%20was%20only, and%20men%20equal%20pension%20benefits (accessed 11 November 2024).

11. 'Gender pensions gap', Now:Pensions, 2024: www.nowpensions.com/about-us/fair-pensions-for-all/gender-pensions-gap/#:~:text=The%202024%20gender%20pensions%20gap%20report%20finds%3A,of%20money%20as%20working%20men (accessed 8 October 2024) and 'Gender pay gap in the UK: 2023', Office for National Statistics: https://commonslibrary.parliament.uk/research-briefings/cbp-9517/ (accessed 8 October 2024).

12. Watson, Erica. '10 reasons to start a business when you're over 50', Prowess: Women In Business, 2023: https://prowess.org.uk/business-over-50#:~:text=Women%20in%20their%202050s%20are,you%20have%20some%20fantastic%20advantages (accessed 8 October 2024).

13. Powell, Caitlin. 'Women hold majority of non-executive board roles for the first time ever, analysis finds', People Management, 2021: www.peoplemanagement.co.uk/article/1747306/women-hold-majority-non-executive-board-roles-first-time-analysis-finds (accessed 8 October 2024).

14. Moffatt, Suzanne. 'Social inclusivity within the University of the Third Age', British Society of Gerontology, 2015: https://ageingissues.wordpress.com/2015/09/04/social-inclusivity-within-the-university-of-the-third-age/ (accessed 8 October 2024).

Chapter 3

1. O'Neil, Deborah, Hopkins, Margaret, and Bilimoria, Diana. 'Women's careers at the start of the 21st century: patterns and paradoxes', *Journal of Business Ethics*, 80(4), 2008, pp. 727–43.

2. O'Neil, Deborah, and Bilimoria, Diana. 'Women's career development phases: idealism, endurance and reinvention', *Career Development International*, 10, 2005, pp. 168–89.

3. Ibid.

4. Mainiero, Lisa, and Sullivan, Sherry. 'Kaleidoscope careers: an alternate explanation for the "opt-out" revolution', *The Academy of Management Executive*, 19(1), 2005, pp. 105–23.

5. Ibid.

6. 'Nature vs nurture: The nature nurture debate', Betterhelp Editorial Team, 2024: www.betterhelp.com/advice/psycho logists/what-is-the-nature-vs-nurture-psychology-debate-and-how-does-it-affect-me/#:~:text=Now%2C%20 it's%20generally%20accepted%20within,influence%20gene-%20expression%20(nature) (accessed 13 November 2024).

7. 'What women want', Centre for Progressive Studies, 2024: www.progressive-policy.net/publications/what-women-want (accessed 13 November 2024).

8. Moffett, Jane. 'Being a working carer', *Workplace*, British Association of Counselling and Psychotherapy, July 2020, pp. 26–8.

9. Stern, Daniel, and Bruschweiler-Stern, Nadia. *The Birth of a Mother: How Motherhood Changes You Forever* (Bloomsbury, 1998).

10. Millward, Lynne. 'The transition to motherhood in an organizational context: an interpretative phenomenological

analysis', 79(3), 2006, pp. 315–33: https://bpspsychub.online library.wiley.com/doi/abs/10.1348/096317906X110322 (accessed 6 August 2024).

11. Prosser, Margaret. 'Shaping a Fairer Future: a review of the recommendations of the Women and Work Commission three years on', for the *Women in Work Commission*, 2009: https://web archive.nationalarchives.gov.uk/ukgwa/20100212235759/ http:/www.equalities.gov.uk/pdf/297158_WWC_Report_acc. pdf (accessed 13 November 2024).

12. Easton, Mark. 'Women still do more housework survey suggests', BBC News, 21 September 2023: www.bbc.co.uk/news/uk-66866879 (accessed 8 October 2024).

13. Moffett, Jane, and Seignot, Nicki. 'Policies and practices through the prism of working parenthood: an analysis of factors that help and hinder the engagement and retention of returning talent post parental leave' (Kangaroo Coaching and the Parent Mentor, 2020).

Chapter 4

1. Ryan, Lucy. *Revolting Women: Why Midlife Women Are Walking Out* (Practical Inspiration Publishing, 2023).

2. Hisliff, Gaby. 'Not just hot flushes: how menopause can destroy mental health', *The Guardian*, 12 January 2023: www.theguardian.com/society/2023/jan/12/not-just-hot-flushes-how-menopause-can-destroy-mental-health (accessed 15 October 2024).

3. 'Menopausal women with zest', Ageless Possibilities, 2020: www.agelesspossibilities.org/blog-1/menopausal-women-with-zest (accessed 15 October 2024).

4. '5 million grandparents take on childcare responsibilities', Age UK, 2017: www.ageuk.org.uk/latest-news/articles/2017/september/five-million-grandparents-take-on-childcare-responsibilities/ (accessed 25 November 2024).

5. 'This Counts as Care Campaign launches', Carers UK, 2024: www.carersuk.org/news/this-counts-as-care-campaign-launches/ (accessed 14 October 2024).

6. Ryan, Lucy. *Revolting Women: Why Midlife Women Are Walking Out* (Practical Inspiration Publishing, 2023).

7. 'Ageing better? Life over 60 in the 21st century', English Longitudinal Study of Ageing, 2023: www.elsa-project.ac.uk/celebrating-elsa (accessed 20 November 2024).

8. Setti, Ilaria, Dordoni, Paola, Piccoli, Beatrice, Bellotto, Massimo, and Argentero, Pergiorgio. 'Proactive personality and training motivation among older workers: a mediational model of goal orientation', *European Journal of Training and Development*, 39(8), 2015, pp. 681–99.

9. Froehlich, Dominik, Raemdonck, Isabel, and Beausaert, Simon. 'Resources to increase older workers' motivation and intention to learn', *Vocations in Learning*, 16, 2022, pp. 47–71.

10. https://noon.org.uk (accessed 25 November 2024).

11. Ryan, Lucy. *Revolting Women: Why Midlife Women Are Walking Out* (Practical Inspiration Publishing, 2023).

12. Van der Horst, Mariska. 'Internalised ageism and self-exclusion: does feeling old and health pessimism make individuals want to retire early?', *Social Inclusion*, 7(3), 2019, pp. 27–43.

Chapter 5

1. Truyens, Marc. 'Transition Theory: Nancy K. Schlossberg 1984', CAREER MARCR for Career Professionals, 2019: https://marcr.net/marcr-for-career-professionals/career-theory/career-theories-and-theorists/transition-theory-nancy-k-schlossberg/ (accessed 4 October 2024).

2. Dodwell, Tessa. 'Coaching needs to differ before and after the transition to retirement', *The International Journal of Coaching and Mentoring*, S14, 2020, pp. 102–18.

3. www.ons.gov.uk/employmentandlabourmarket/peopleinwork/employmentandemployeetypes/articles/peopleaged65yearsandoverinemploymentuk/januarytomarch2022toapriltojune2022 (accessed 23 July 2024).

Chapter 6

1. Gratton, Lynda, and Scott, Andrew J. *The 100-Year Life: Living and Working in an Age of Longevity* (Bloomsbury, 2020).

2. Keightley, Samuel, Duncan, Myanna, and Gardner, Benjamin. 'Working from home during lockdown may have impacted health behaviours', Kings College London News Centre, 2022: www.kcl.ac.uk/news/research-shows-working-from-home-during-lockdown-may-have-impacted-health-behaviours (accessed 12 July 2024).

3. 'Unveiling the vital connection between routine and mental health': www.generalandmedical.com/live-healthy/posts/2023/october/routine-for-your-mental-health/ (accessed 27 November 2024).

Chapter 7

1. Gratton, Lynda, and Scott, Andrew J. *The 100-Year Life: Living and Working in an Age of Longevity* (Bloomsbury, 2020).

2. Cunnington, Ross. 'Neuroplasticity: how the brain changes with learning', IBE Science of Learning Portal, 2019: https://solportal.ibe-unesco.org/articles/neuroplasticity-how-the-brain-changes-with-learning/ (accessed 2 December 2024).

3. Sethi, Bhushan, Brown, Peter, and Zhao, Yalin. 'Younger workers want training, flexibility and transparency', Strategy + Business, PWC, 2022: www.strategy-business.com/article/Younger-workers-want-training-flexibility-and-transparency (accessed 27 November 2024).

4. Froehlich, Dominik, Raemdonck, Isabel, and Beausaert, Simon. 'Resources to increase older workers' motivation and intention to learn', *Vocations in Learning*, 16, 2022, pp. 47–71.

5. 'Grow your brain', Department for Continuing Education, University of Oxford: www.conted.ox.ac.uk/about/brain-resources (accessed 2 December 2024).

6. Ryan, Lucy. *Revolting Women: Why Midlife Women Are Walking Out* (Practical Inspiration Publishing, 2023).

Chapter 8

1. Steinem, Gloria. BBC Radio 4 *Woman's Hour*, 11 April 2024.

2. Buettner, Dan. *Live to 100: Secrets of the Blue Zones*, Netflix, 2023: www.netflix.com/title/81214929.

3. Gratton, Lynda, and Scott, Andrew J. *The 100-Year Life: Living and Working in an Age of Longevity* (Bloomsbury, 2020).

4. Lewis, Thomas, Amini Fari, and Lannon, Richard. *A General Theory of Love* (Vintage, 2001).

5. Mosley, Michael. 'Just one thing: reach out', BBC Radio 4: www.bbc.co.uk/programmes/articles/3k4DPSzMH72HHzzpgT2D8k6/can-reaching-out-to-a-friend-or-neighbour-make-you-healthier (accessed 12 July 2024).

6. Steven, Claire. '5 things you can do now to reduce dementia risk', Zoe Science and Nutrition podcast, 2024: www.youtube.com/watch?v=N_hN2OlkMCg (accessed 2 December 2024).

7. 'Ageing better? Life over 60 in the 21st century', English Longitudinal Study of Ageing, 2023: www.elsa-project.ac.uk/celebrating-elsa (accessed 20 November 2024).

8. Fasbender, Ulrike, Wang, Mo, Voltmer, Jan Bennet, and Deller, Jurgen. 'The meaning of work for post-retirement employment decisions', *Work, Aging and Retirement*, 2(1), 2016, pp. 12–23.

9. 'What is a grey divorce? 5 things you should know about separating later in life', Progression Solicitors: www.progressionsolicitors.com/what-is-a-grey-divorce-5-things-you-should-know-about-separating-in-later-life/#:~:text=Many%20factors%20can%20contribute%20to,about%20a%20'grey%20divorce' (accessed 13 July 2024).

Chapter 9

1. Gratton, Lynda, and Scott, Andrew J. *The 100-Year Life: Living and Working in an Age of Longevity* (Bloomsbury, 2020).

2. Ryan, Lucy. *Revolting Women: Why Midlife Women Are Walking Out* (Practical Inspiration Publishing, 2023).

3. Mosconi, Lisa. 'Imaging study reveals brain changes during the transition to menopause', Weill Cornell Medicine, 2021:

https://news.weill.cornell.edu/news/2021/06/imaging-study-reveals-brain-changes-during-the-transition-to-menopause (accessed 26 November 2024).

4. Kristjansson, Clarissa. 'Traditional Chinese medicine and rebirth', MenoClarity, 2022: https://menoclarity.com/traditional-chinese-medicine-menopause/ (accessed 26 November 2024).

5. Karpen, Ruth Ray. 'Reflections on women's retirement', *The Gerontologist*, 57(1), 2017, pp. 103–9.

6. Rochon, Paula, Kalia, Surbhi, and Higgs, Paul. 'Gendered ageism: addressing discrimination based on age and sex', *The Lancet*, 398(10301), 2021, pp. 648–69.

Chapter 10

1. Hill, Amelia. '"Keeping horrors of old age at bay": octogenarian workers defy stereotypes', *The Guardian*, 27 December 2023: www.theguardian.com/society/2023/dec/27/keeping-horrors-of-old-age-at-bay-octogenarian-workers-defy-stereotypes (accessed 8 November 2024).

2. Buettner, Dan. *Live to 100: Secrets of the Blue Zones*, Netflix, 2023: www.netflix.com/title/81214929.

3. García, Héctor, and Miralles, Francesc. *Ikigai: The Japanese Secret to a Long and Happy Life* (Hutchinson, 2017).

4. Gander, Kashmira. 'People with a sense of purpose live longer, study suggests', Newsweek, 2019: www.newsweek.com/people-sense-purpose-live-longer-study-suggests-1433771 (accessed 2 December 2024).

5. Gratton, Lynda, and Scott, Andrew J. *The 100-Year Life: Living and Working in an Age of Longevity* (Bloomsbury, 2020).

6. 'People aged 65 years and over in employment, UK: January to March 2022 to April to June 2022', Census 2021, ONS, 2022: www.ons.gov.uk/employmentandlabourmarket/peopleinwork/employmentandempltojune2022 (accessed 23 July 2024).

7. 'Career anchors – Edgar Schein': www.businessballs.com/self-management/career-anchors-edgar-schein/ (accessed 29 October 2024).

8. García, Héctor, and Miralles, Francesc. *Ikigai: The Japanese Secret to a Long and Happy Life* (Hutchinson, 2017).

Section 3

1. *Blue Peter*, BBC: www.bbc.co.uk/cbbc/shows/blue-peter.

Index

4S Model 19–21, 54
55/Redefined 108
100-Year Life, The (Gratton and Scott) 6–7, 81, 92, 93, 96, 124

A
acceptance and integration/commitment stage (Change Curve) 17–18
age
  leaving work decision factor 55
  perceptions of 105–106, 107–109
Age UK 45
Ageing Better? Life over 60 in the 21st Century, English Longitudinal Study of Ageing, 2023 47, 94
ageism 108
  gendered 3, 43, 48–49, 108–109
  internalized 49
  midlife collision 43, 47–49
Allen, Carol 120
anger and depression stage (Change Curve) 17
artistic and creative activities 88, 102, 120
  see also hobbies
authenticity 34, 61–62, 107
Autonomy/independence (Career Anchor) 125

B
babies
  need for social contact 92
  see also childcare responsibilities
bias, and workplace sex discrimination 27
Birth of a Mother, The (Stern and Bruschweiler-Stern) 37
Blue Zones 7, 91, 120
boundaries, between work and home 71

'boundaryless' careers 33–34
brain, the
  and learning 82
  menopausal and post-menopausal changes 106
'breathing space' years 8
Bridges, William, Bridges' Transition Model 18–19
Bruschweiler-Stern, Nadia 37
Buettner, Dan 120

C
campaigning groups 103
Career Anchors 125–127, 130, 133
career breaks 30
Carers UK 36, 45
caring responsibilities 29–30, 35–36, 45, 73
  working carers 36
  see also childcare responsibilities; elderly relatives; partners
Change Curve 16–18
change, difference from transition 18
childcare costs 98
childcare responsibilities 29–30, 35, 38–41, 56, 98, 123
children, impact on women's careers 34–35
circadian rhythm 72
coaching 66–67
colleagues, social relationships with 94–96
commitment *see* acceptance and integration/commitment stage (Change Curve)
connection 9, 81–82, 85–87
  map 132, 136, 142
  need for 92–94
  see also relationships
consultancy work 110
continued professional development 84
control, over leaving work 54, 61, 62
COVID-19 pandemic 43
  impact on leaving work 46–47, 55–56
  women's mental health 71
  workplace relationships 95
creative people 84
culture, and workplace sex discrimination 27, 28

D
dementia 83, 93
denial *see* shock and denial stage (Change Curve)
depression *see* anger and depression stage (Change Curve); mental health
developmental psychology, of women 33
divorce 99–101
'doing it all' 29–30

E
education, sex discrimination in 26
elderly relatives, caring responsibilities 36, 45–46, 56, 70, 98–99
'elegant exit' 53, 60

'Empowered Women: From
    Retired to Redefined'
    courses 7–8, 16, 83, 86,
    94, 97, 121
'empty chair' exercise 63–64
empty nest syndrome 100
ending, losing and letting
    go phase, Bridges'
    Transition Model 18, 21
English Longitudinal Study of
    Ageing 47, 94
Entrepreneurial creativity
    (Career Anchor) 125
entrepreneurs, women 31,
    124–125
Equal Pay Act 1970 27

F
family relationships 98–99
family responsibilities
  impact on women's careers
    34–35, 36–38
  see also childcare
    responsibilities;
    elderly relatives, caring
    responsibilities; partners
female role models 28–29, 49
'filling time' 119
financial factors 30
  divorce 100
  gender pay gap 27
  post-retirement paid work 124
  see also pensions
flexible working, lack of for
    working mothers 40
'flow' state 120, 128–129
friends, social relationships
    with 96–97

G
García, Héctor 122, 129
gender pay gap 27
gendered ageism 3, 43, 48–49,
    108–109
General management
    competence (Career
    Anchor) 125
generational context, women's
    generational experiences
    5, 23–26
'giving back' 123, 130
glass ceiling 28
grandmothers 45, 56, 98,
    107–108
Gratton, Lynda 6–7, 81, 92, 93,
    96, 124
'grey divorce' 99
growth 9, 81–82
  map 132, 136, 142
  see also learning

H
'having it all' 29–30
health
  impact of leaving work on 55
  loneliness 93–94
  routines 72
healthcare practices, gendered
    ageism 108
higher education, women's
    access to 26, 27
hobbies 69, 88, 102, 123
  see also artistic and creative
    activities
'holding' space 71
home working, lack of for
    working mothers 40

household responsibilities 29–30, 39
hybrid working, and workplace relationships 95

I
identity and image 10, 25–26, 109–111, 114–117
  changing the narrative around 111–113
  grandmothers 107–108
  map 132–133, 138, 144
  motherhood 37–38
  see also status; Strategies (4S Model)
ikigai 87, 120–122, 123, 127, 128–129, 133
imposter syndrome 28
income *see* financial factors; pensions
'intangible assets' 7, 66, 81, 92–93, 96, 124
integration *see* acceptance and integration/commitment stage (Change Curve)
invisibility, of older women 108–109

J
juvenescence 7, 105–106

K
kaleidoscope careers 34
Karpen, Ruth Ray 106–107
Kubler-Ross, Elizabeth, Change Curve 16–18

L
Lancet, The 108
learning 9, 81–83
  benefits of 82–83
  learning goal motivation 83
  map 132, 136, 142
  in practice 83–85
Learning and Development departments, training needs of older workers 47–48
leaving work 9, 53, 56–57, 60–64
  age as a factor in 55
  caring responsibilities 45
  childcare responsibilities 40–41
  COVID-19 pandemic 46–47, 55–56
  'elegant exit' 53, 60
  external factors 56
  financial factors 56–57
  making the decision 53–57
  map 132, 134, 140
  negative effects of 16, 54, 114
  phased endings 59
  reasons for 20, 55
  terminology 2
  timing 58–60
  see also psychological transition of leaving work
life expectancy
  increases in 6, 7, 45, 98–99, 105, 124
  and purpose 122
Lifestyle (Career Anchor) 126
loneliness, and health 93–94

loss 16, 18–19
  see also ending, losing and letting go phase, Bridges' Transition Model

M
male role models 28
map exercise 131–145
marriage bar 23–24
maternity leave 30
Mead, Margaret 34
meaning 10, 96, 119–120
  map 133, 139, 145
  see also ikigai
men
  gendered approach to retirement 1, 3
  male role models 28
  perceptions of older men 109
menopause 43–44
  see also post-menopause
mental health 91
mentoring 110, 123
midlife collision 43–47
  and ageism 43, 47–49
Mills, Eleanor 48
Milward, Lynne 37
Miralles, Francesc 122, 129
motherhood
  impact on women's careers 34–35, 36–38
  psychological transition 37–39
motivation 118
  and learning 82–83

N
nature-nurture debate 35

neuroscience 82
neutral zone phase, Bridges' Transition Model 18, 21
new beginnings phase, Bridges' Transition Model 18
non-executive directorships 31, 123
Noon 48
notice periods 58–59
nurseries 29

O
Okinawa, Japan 120

P
paid work, post-retirement 124–125
partners 99–101
  caring responsibilities for 36, 46, 56
part-time work 39, 41, 55, 57, 59, 98, 114, 124
  childcare responsibilities 34–35, 40–41
pensions 30
  retirement ages 24, 25
  see also financial factors
Pensions Acts 24
personal values 121, 129
'portfolio careers' 124
post-menopause 106–107
'post-menopausal zest' 34, 44
productive assets 7
Prosser, Margaret. 39
psychological transition of leaving work 8–9, 15–16, 18

4S Model 19–21, 54
Bridges' Transition Model 18–19
Change Curve 16–18
Pure challenge (Career Anchor) 126
purpose 10, 30–31, 119–120
  and learning 85
  map 133, 139, 145
  see also ikigai

R
redundancy 60
'regenerative friendships' 96
relationism 33–34
relationships 9, 91–92, 102–103
  colleagues 94–96
  family 98–99
  friends 96–97
  importance of in women's developmental psychology 33
  map 132, 137, 143
  need for social connection 92–94
  partners 99–101
  see also Support (4S Model)
relevance, desire to maintain 85, 86
retirement
  as a concept 1–2
  gendered approach to 1, 3, 5
  terminology 2
retirement ages 24, 25
Revolting Women: Why Midlife Women Are Walking Out, and what to do about it (Ryan) 48–49, 84
routines, and health 72
Ryan, Lucy 43, 48–49, 84

S
safety 1–2, 71
Schein, Edgar 125
Schlossberg, Nancy, 4S Model 19–21
Scott, Andrew 6–7, 81, 92, 93, 96, 124
seclusion 1, 2
second shift 29–30
Security/stability (Career Anchor) 125
Self (4S Model) 19, 20
self-employment 53, 57, 125
self-image *see* identity and image; Strategies (4S Model)
Service/dedication to a cause (Career Anchor) 126
Sex Discrimination Act 1975 24, 26–30
'Shaping a Fairer Future: a review of the recommendations of the Women and Work Commission three years on,' Margaret Prosser for the *Women in Work Commission*, 2009: 39
shock and denial stage (Change Curve) 17
'silver foxes' 109
'silver splitters' 99

Simpson, Lindsey 108
Situation (4S Model) 19, 20, 54
status 10, 25–26, 41, 109, 113–116
  map 132–133, 138, 144
  see also identity and image
Steinem, Gloria 91
Steptoe, Andrew 93–94
Stern, Daniel 37
Strategies (4S Model) 19, 20
structure 9, 65–66, 68, 71–74
  map 132, 135, 141
  Wheel of Life exercise 77–78
'superagers' 93
Support (4S Model) 19, 20
Sweden, childcare 98

T
Technical/functional competence (Career Anchor) 125, 126
time 9, 65–66, 67–70
  of leaving work 58–60
  map 132, 135, 141
  Wheel of Life exercise 76–77
'time of redefinition' terminology 2
training
  menopause policies 44, 106
  older workers' needs 47–48
transformational assets 7
transition
  difference from change 18
  see also psychological transition of leaving work
'twilight years' 7, 106

U
U3A (University of the Third Age) 31
universities, women's access to 26, 27

V
vitality assets 7
volunteering 89, 115, 123, 127

W
Wheel of Life exercise 76–79
Women and Work Commission: 'Shaping a Fairer Future: a review of the recommendations of the Women and Work Commission three years on,' Margaret Prosser for the *Women in Work Commission,* 2009: 39
women entrepreneurs 31, 124–125
women's careers 33–35
  caring responsibilities 29–30, 35–36, 45, 73
  childcare responsibilities 29–30, 35, 38–41, 56, 98, 123
  family responsibilities 34–35, 36–41
  late-career stage 34
  phases in 34
  women's career development theory 9, 107

workplace
  menopause policies 44
  sex discrimination in 27–28

Y
'younger for longer' concept
    6–7, 105

Z
zero-hours contracts 57

A quick word from Practical Inspiration Publishing...

We hope you found this book both practical and inspiring – that's what we aim for with every book we publish.

We publish titles on topics ranging from leadership, entrepreneurship, HR and marketing to self-development and wellbeing.

Find details of all our books at: www.practicalinspiration.com

 Did you know...

We can offer discounts on bulk sales of all our titles – ideal if you want to use them for training purposes, corporate giveaways or simply because you feel these ideas deserve to be shared with your network.

We can even produce bespoke versions of our books, for example with your organization's logo and/or a tailored foreword.

To discuss further, contact us on info@practicalinspiration.com.

 **Got an idea for a business book?**

We may be able to help. Find out more about publishing in partnership with us at: bit.ly/PIpublishing.

Follow us on social media...

 @PIPTalking

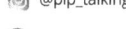 @pip_talking

@practicalinspiration

@piptalking

Practical Inspiration Publishing

www.ingramcontent.com/pod-product-compliance
Lightning Source LLC
Chambersburg PA
CBHW032226080426
42735CB00008B/739